Documents and Questi

BRITISH HISTORY
1815-1914

Peter Lane

Formerly Head of the History Department,
Coloma College of Education, West Wickham, Kent

John Murray

Also by Peter Lane

Success in British History 1760-1914 (John Murray)
British Social and Economic History from 1760 to the Present Day (OUP)

The editor and publishers have found it necessary to shorten some of the documents. Great care has been taken to ensure that the meaning has not been obscured or distorted, and no other changes have been made to the original wording.

Acknowledgements

The editor and publishers would like to thank the following who have kindly permitted the reproduction of copyright photographs:

BBC Hulton Picture Library (pp. 16, 49, 61, 64); B. T. Batsford/ *Punch* (p. 57); Crown Copyright, National Railway Museum, York (p. 19); Dudley Public Libraries (p. 13); William Gordon Davis (pp. 22, 63); Glasgow University Library (p. 2); Greater London Council (p. 75); Mansell Collection (pp. 3, 7, 8, 14, 15, 23, 82); *Punch* (pp. 13, 27, 33, 35, 48, 50, 52, 55, 58, 77, ,78, 84, 88); The Salvation Army (pp. 44, 72); Staffordshire Records Office (p. 26); TUC (pp. 38, 41); British Rail Western Region (cover).

Acknowledgements and thanks are also due to the following for permission to reproduce copyright material:

Hutchinson, *Memories and Reflections* by Ben Tillett (p. 68); Macmillan, *Life of Joseph Chamberlain* by J. L. Garvin and J. Amery (pp. 61, 85, 86); Eveleigh Nash, *My Own Story* by E. Pankhurst (p. 66); Newnes, *My Life's Battles* by W. Thorne (p. 42); Nicholson and Watson, *An Autobiography* by Viscount Snowden (pp. 70, 71); Thornton, Butterworth, *The World Crisis* by Winston Churchill (pp. 78, 87, 89).

Printed in Great Britain by Martin's of Berwick

British Library Cataloguing in Publication Data

Lane, Peter
  Documents and questions.
  Vol. 2: British history 1815-1914
  1. Great Britain – History – Sources
  I. Title
  941.07   DA470

ISBN 0-7195-3775-4

Introduction

In these three books of documents I have tried to give the student a 'flavour' of history that cannot be given in the straightforward textbook. It is valuable for us to read contemporary accounts—of the conditions of the roads in the eighteenth century, the way in which parliamentary elections were conducted in the days before reform, or the political crisis which split the Labour government in 1931.

Reading these documents and examining contemporary illustrations will also help the student to understand the nature of the work of both the historian and the authors of history textbooks. Understanding and 'getting behind the book' will, I trust, make the study of history more enjoyable and more worthwhile.

It is also possible to give, in documentary form, information which a textbook simply cannot provide. It is worth reading the details of the India Act of 1784 or the Education Act of 1870 or the Budget of 1931 — important issues which most textbooks can only summarise.

I have concentrated on those major topics which have to be studied and on which examination questions will continue to be set. I am grateful to the publishers who have devised a format which has enabled me to present a number of documents on each topic. This permits a study of several features of each. Thus in Book 1 the question of enclosures is seen from the point of view of the landowner who gained from them, the commoner who lost by them, and the population at large whose food would not have been supplied without them. In Book 2 the arguments over such major issues as home rule for Ireland and the changing nature of Liberalism after 1880 are examined. In Book 3 there are a number of documents on the economic problems which led to the onset of the great depression of the 1920s, and on the social effects on individuals and families of the large-scale unemployment which accompanied it.

Most examination boards now include a question or questions based on documentary material, written or illustrative. Each of these three books contains the kind of material that has been used in past examinations and will no doubt be used again in the future.

Contents

(Items in italics are illustrations.)

Topic 1 Britain and Europe, 1815–1830

1 The postwar slump

A transition from war to peace must always affect several branches of public wealth, some connected with foreign, but a greater proportion with domestic trade. Two departments of industry have suffered severely by the cessation of hostilities; the provision trade of Ireland and the manufacture of arms at Birmingham. The distress arising from the peace in those branches of commerce may be temporary; if all the other channels of trade, unconnected with the war, were open, it certainly would be temporary. But when we find the depression general in all lines of employment, in those uninfluenced by the war-demand, as well as in those wholly dependent upon it, we are driven to the conclusion that the return of peace accounts only for a portion of the sad change we everywhere witness. The cotton trade, wholly unconnected with the war, is more depressed than the iron trade in general and gun manufactory at Birmingham. I conclude, first, that the transition from war to peace has not produced all the mischief; and next, that the mischief which it has produced might have been got over, as in former time, if it had been the only one which oppressed us. Sir, we must once for all look our situation in the face and firmly take a view of the extent of our disease.

(Henry Brougham in the House of Commons, 13 March 1817)

2 Taxation

Taxes upon every article which enters into the mouth, or covers the back, or is placed under the foot—on everything that comes from abroad or is grown at home—taxes on the raw material—taxes on every fresh value that is added to it by the industry of man—on the ermine which decorates the judge, and the rope which hangs the criminal—on the poor man's salt and the rich man's spice—on the brass nails of the coffin, and the ribands of the bride—at bed or board, couchant or levant, we must pay. The dying Englishman flings himself back upon his chintz bed which has paid twenty two per cent—makes his will on an eight pound stamp, and expires in the arms of an apothecary who has paid a licence of £100 for the privilege of putting him to death. His whole property is then immediately taxed from two to ten per cent. Beside the probate, large fees are demanded for burying him in the chancel; his virtues are handed down to posterity on taxed marble, and he is then gathered to his fathers—to be taxed no more.

(Sydney Smith, *The Edinburgh Review*, 1820)

[1]

1 In which year was *the cessation of hostilities*?
2 Why did the Birmingham arms trade suffer severely from the *transition from war to peace*? Name two other industries which suffered for the same reason.
3 Why was the cotton trade depressed? Do you agree that its depression was *wholly unconnected with the war*? Why?
4 Brougham said *the transition from war to peace has not produced all the mischief*. What were the other reasons for the depressed state of industry and for high unemployment?
5 What was the Government's policy towards (i) the trade depression, and (ii) the unemployed?
6 When did the postwar depression come to an end? What led to this improvement in the economic situation?

[2]

1 Why was taxation at a high level in 1820? How far was this the result of the Napoleonic Wars?
2 Smith complained of the high level of indirect taxes. What is the difference between direct and indirect taxation? Why was there little direct tax in 1820?
3 Explain why indirect taxation affected the poor man more than the rich. How did this taxation affect the standard of living of poorer people? Why did this taxation lead to a lower demand for British goods?
4 When, how and by whom was indirect taxation first lowered?

3 The suspension of Habeas Corpus, 1817

The petitions to Parliament from the different agricultural interests were numerous this year [1816]. The manufacturers at the same time complained of want of employment due to the general impoverishment of their countrymen; riots arose in the inland counties. At the close of the year a popular meeting took place in Spa-fields, Islington, and resolutions of reform, suggested by Mr. Henry Hunt, were voted by acclamation. The rioters carried off fire-arms from the shops of several gunsmiths. The mob marched to the Royal Exchange, where they had a short contest with the Lord Mayor.

At the opening of Parliament in 1817 on the return of the Prince from the House of Peers, an immense crowd had assembled, by whom he was received with demonstrations of discontent and anger; the glass of the carriage was broken by a stone. This flagrant outrage being on the same day reported by Lord Sidmouth to Parliament, the two Houses joined in an address suitable to the occasion; and voted the offer of £1000 reward for the discovery of the offender. On the 24th [February] a motion was made by Lord Sidmouth in the Upper House for a suspension of the Habeas Corpus Act until the 1st of July ensuing. Lord Liverpool remarked, that 'They had, according to their report, proofs of a system to overthrow the constitution of the country. He felt the necessity of preserving to every man his fire-side, and on these grounds he asked, for a very short time, the powers which were indispensable to the salvation of the State.'

(*Memoirs of the Rt Hon. The Earl of Liverpool*, 1827)

[3]
1 What reason is given in this extract for the *want of employment*? Give three reasons for the high unemployment in 1817.
2 In what ways did the people show their dissatisfaction?
3 What, in particular, did Hunt wish to reform? Why?
4 Why did the *Prince* and not the King open Parliament in 1817?
5 What government post was occupied by Lord Sidmouth? Name two other members of Liverpool's Government in 1817.
6 What powers did the Government gain by *a suspension of the Habeas Corpus Act*?
7 What other repressive Acts were passed in this period 1815–22?

4 The Dance of Life

[4]
1 Why was poaching so widespread in 1817? Why did the people not buy the food they needed?
2 How had landowners used their political power to get poaching made illegal? Give one other example of the way in which they used their political power for their own benefit.
3 What job was done by the man holding the dead animal?
4 Why were many landowners also magistrates? How did this help them to combat the habit of poaching?
5 Why were poachers punished less severely after 1825 than they had been before that date?

5 Peterloo, 1819

'Stand fast,' I said, 'they are riding upon us.'

The cavalry were in confusion; they could not, with all the weight of man and horse, penetrate that compact mass of human beings, and their sabres were plied to hew a way through naked held-up hands and defenceless heads; and then chopped limbs and wound-gaping skulls were seen, and cries and groans were mingled with the din of that horrid confusion. 'For shame! For shame!' was shouted. Then 'Break! Break! They are killing them in front and they cannot get away.' For a moment the crowd held back as in a pause, then there was a rush, heavy and resistless as a headlong sea, and a sound like low thunder, with screams, prayers and imprecations from the sabre-doomed crowd who could not escape. On the crowd breaking the yeomanry wheeled, and, dashing whenever there was an opening, they rode, pressing and wounding. Women, maids and tender youths were indiscriminately sabred or trampled. In ten minutes from the beginning of the havoc the field was an almost deserted space. The hustings remained, with a few broken flag staves and a torn banner or two, whilst over the whole field were strewed caps, bonnets, hats, shawls and shoes all trampled, torn and bloody. The yeomanry had dismounted—some were easing their horses' girths, others adjusting their accoutrements, and some were wiping their sabres. Several mounds of human beings were where they had fallen, crushed down.

(Samuel Bamford, *Passages in the Life of a Radical*, 1844)

[5]

1 Who ordered the charge of the cavalry? Why did they do so?

2 Who was the main speaker at this meeting? How was he punished for his part in this demonstration?

3 What reform did the people hope for? Why did this seem so important to them at the time?

4 When and where did this meeting take place? Why was it later given the name 'Peterloo'?

5 How did the Government behave when it heard of this attack? Why?

6 What Acts were passed just after this to forbid any more such meetings?

6 Castlereagh and Canning

The Grand Assembly of Crowned Heads and Ministers at the Congress of Vienna, almost wholly occupied in their own aggrandizement, either neglected to take measures for preserving future tranquillity, or betrayed ignorance of public feeling. Civilised nations are not now willing to be transferred from sovereign to sovereign like the slaves of Africa. Who is there that thinks the Poles can be satisfied with their country having been rendered a province of Russia?

The Allies had publicly proclaimed the restoration of the *status quo* in Europe, if its different nations assisted them in overthrowing Buonaparte. On the fulfilment of this pledge, the Marquis of Londonderry should have insisted. We formerly traded with the States which were parcelled out at the Congress of Vienna; and if they had been placed on their ancient and independent footing, Great Britain would have immediately resumed her commercial relations with them. But instead of this, the partitioned States are incorporated with Governments who have prohibited or restricted our commerce.

The discerning mind of Mr. Canning will, doubtless draw the true conclusions from the scene. He is not personally connected with any of the Foreign Courts, nor personally pledged to their measures. The adoption of a new line of policy by him does not carry with it the painful acknowledgment that his former system had been wrong.

(Lewis Goldsmith, *Observations on the Appointment of the Rt Hon. Geo. Canning,* 1822)

7 British Foreign Policy

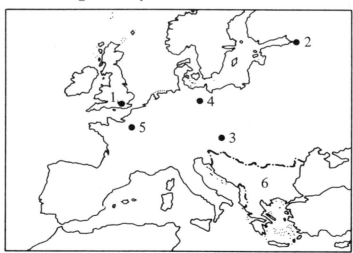

[6]

1 Which *Crowned Heads and Ministers* represented the Allies at the Congress of Vienna? Who represented France at that Congress?

2 What is meant by *aggrandizement*? What territorial gains were made at Vienna by the Allies? What gains had Britain made as a result of the Napoleonic Wars?

3 Explain *status quo*. Why did the Allies not honour the pledges which had been given?

4 By what name is *the Marquis of Londonderry* better known? How had he failed to look after British *commercial* interests?

5 Why did Goldsmith think that it would be easier for Mr Canning to adopt a different foreign policy?

6 How, by 1822, had Castlereagh shown that he had become opposed to the policies of *the Foreign Courts*?

7 How did Canning look after British *commercial* interests and oppose *the Foreign Courts* over the former Spanish colonies in South America?

[7]

When answering the questions, choose the most appropriate of the numbers on the map as your answer *and* name the place or country concerned.

1 Which city was occupied by foreign armies between 1815 and 1818? Why?

2 Which capitals were linked by the Quadruple Alliance?

3 Where did the two rulers who did not sign the Holy Alliance live?

4 To which city did Hardenberg return after the Congress of Vienna?

5 Which city was the centre of the most polyglot Empire?

6 In which city was there a coronation ceremony in 1825?

7 Which country did Castlereagh and Metternich wish to see neutralised? Why?

8 In which capital was a treaty signed in 1827 in an attempt to solve the Greek question?

8 Peel and the Metropolitan Police

(a)

Letter from Peel to Wellington, 29 May 1829

I send you the Report of the Committee of last year on the Police of the Metropolis. In 1822 there were 2,539 committals; in 1825, 2,902; and in 1828, 3,516. This is a strong proof of the rapid increase of crime, and the necessity of some effectual measures for its repression. In 1822 there were 12 committals for breaking into a dwelling house; in 1825, 23; and in 1828, 102.

The paper marked A contains a list of parishes in which the watch establishment is defective. Just conceive the state of one parish, in which there are eighteen different boards for the management of the watch, each acting without concert with the other!

The paper marked B contains a list of parishes, in the immediate vicinity of London, in which there is absolutely no watch at all. Think of the state of Brentford and Deptford, with no sort of police by night!

My Bill enables the Secretary of State to abolish gradually the existing watch arrangements, and to substitute in their room a police force that shall act by night and day, under the control of two magistrates. I propose to substitute the new police gradually for the old one, not to attempt too much at first; to begin perhaps with ten or fifteen parishes in the centre of the City of Westminster, and gradually to extend the police district.

(*Sir Robert Peel*, edited C. S. Parker, vol. 2, 1899)

(b)

Letter from Peel to Wellington, 5 November 1829

I am very glad indeed to hear that you think well of the Police. It has given me from the first to last more trouble than anything I undertook.

I want to teach people that liberty does not consist in having your house robbed by organised gangs of thieves, and in leaving the principal streets of London in the nightly possession of drunken women and vagabonds.

The chief danger of the failure of the new system will be, if it is made a job, if gentlemen's servants and so forth are placed in the higher offices.

(*Sir Robert Peel*, edited C. S. Parker)

(c)

Letter from Peel to J. W. Croker MP, 10 October 1829

No doubt three shillings a day will not give me all the virtues under heaven, but I do not want them . . . I have good reasons for thinking that one of my police constables, if a single man, can find out of his pay of a guinea a week: (1) lodgings, (2) medical attendance, (3) very comfortable subsistence at his mess, (4) clothing, and can, after finding these, save, out of his pay, ten shillings a week.

(*The Croker Papers*, edited L. J. Jennings, 1884)

[8]

1 What office did Peel have in the Government in 1829? Who had first appointed him to that office? When? Why had he resigned office in 1827?

2 What office did Wellington have in 1829? When did he first take that post? Whom did he succeed?

3 Why was the police system so ineffective before 1829?

4 Why did Peel propose to change the system *gradually*?

5 Why did Peel think that *a guinea a week* was a sufficient wage for a policeman? What does this tell you about wage rates in general?

6 Why did Peel have *more trouble* when trying to found his Police Force?

7 How did Peel try to reform (i) the legal system, and (ii) British prisons? Give the name of one person on whose work he relied in each case.

Topic 2 Parliamentary Reform, 1830–1832

1 The unreformed system, 1793

The members for the 52 counties are all elected by one uniform right. Every man throughout England, possessed of 40 shillings per annum freehold [land], is entitled to a vote for the County in which such freehold is situated.

With respect to the different cities, towns and boroughs, the right of voting shows an infinite diversity of peculiar customs. In some places the number of voters is limited to a select body not exceeding 30 or 40; in others it is extended to 8,000 or 10,000. In some places the freeman must be a resident, in others his presence is only required at an election.

The remaining rights of voting are of a still more complicated description. Burgageholds, Leaseholds, householders, inhabitants at large, potwallopers and commonalty, each in different boroughs prevail and create endless misunderstandings. In some places the choice of two members belongs to the possessor of a spot of ground where neither houses nor inhabitants have been seen for years.

(A Report for the Society of the Friends of the Poor, 9 February 1793)

[1]
1 How many MPs were elected in each county election? Why did this lead to under-representation in Yorkshire and over-representation in Rutlandshire?
2 What was the qualification to vote in county elections before 1832? How did some landowners gain control of a large block of votes in the areas which they owned?
3 What was the meaning of (i) *freeman*, (ii) *potwalloper*?
4 Why was it easier for candidates to influence the result in some constituencies than in others?
5 What sort of borough is described in the last sentence of the extract? How, if at all, did such a borough differ from a pocket borough?

2 Corruption in the old system

Some seats are private property . . . the right of voting belongs to a few householders . . . and these votes are commanded by the owner of the estate. The fewer they are, the more easily they are managed. A great part of a borough in the west was consumed some years ago by fire, and the lord of the manor would not suffer the houses to be rebuilt for this reason. If such an estate is to be sold, it is advertised as carrying the power of returning two members. Government hold many of these boroughs, and individuals buy others. In this manner are a majority of the members returned.

Where the number of voters is greater the business is more difficult, and expensive. The candidate must deal individually with the constituents, who sell themselves to the highest bidder. Remember that an oath against bribery is required! A common mode of evading the oath is a wager. 'I will bet so much,' says the agent of the candidate, 'that you do not vote for us.' 'Done,' says the voter . . . goes to vote and returns to receive the money, not as the price of his suffrage, but as the bet.

(Richard Southey, *Letters from England*, 1807)

[2]
1 What evidence is there in this extract and in item 1 that only a minority of the adult male population were entitled to vote before 1832?
2 Why did *the lord of the manor* not allow *the houses to be rebuilt*?
3 Who bought boroughs when they came up for sale? Why?
4 How effective was the oath against bribery?
5 Why were some elections expensive? Why were many MPs elected without any opposition?

3 Macaulay's arguments in favour of moderate reform

But, Sir, every argument which would induce me to oppose universal suffrage induces me to support the plan which is now before us. I am opposed to universal suffrage, because it would produce a destructive revolution. I support this plan; I am sure it is our best security against a revolution.

That we may exclude those whom it is necessary to exclude, we must admit those whom it may be safe to admit. At present we oppose the schemes of revolutionaries with only one quarter of our proper force. We say that it is not by mere numbers, but by property and intelligence that the nation ought to be governed. Yet we exclude great masses of property and intelligence. We do more. We drive over to the side of revolution those whom we shut out from power.

History is full of revolutions produced by causes similar to those now operating in England. A portion of the community expands and becomes strong. It demands a place in the system, suited to its present power. If this is granted, all is well. If this is refused, then comes the struggle between the young energy of one class and the ancient privileges of another. Such is the struggle which the middle classes in England are maintaining against an aristocracy . . . or the owner of a ruined hovel [who have] powers which are withheld from cities renowned for the marvels of their wealth and of their industry.

(T. B. Macaulay MP in the House of Commons, 2 March 1831)

4 An election handbill

MR. MANGLES respectfully requests those of his worthy Friends, who may be disposed to celebrate his return to Parliament by their own fire sides as on the last occasion to send the inclosed Dinner Ticket, on or before THURSDAY the 2d of APRIL next, to his Agent MR. G. S. SMALLPEICE who will in exchange for such Ticket, give the Bearer thereof an Order for

TWELVE POUNDS OF BEEF,
ONE GALLON OF STRONG BEER,
TWO QUARTERN LOAVES,
THREE POUNDS AND A HALF OF FLOUR,
TWO POUNDS OF SUET,
TWO POUNDS OF RAISINS,
ONE POUND OF CURRANTS,
AND
TWO BOTTLES OF WINE, (PORT OR SHERRY).

MR. MANGLES also begs respectfully to inform those Friends who may not feel disposed to dine in public, and may not wish themselves to exchange the Dinner Ticket, that the same is transferrable to any of their Neighbors.

An Answer is respectfully requested to be sent to MR. G. S. SMALLPEICE, on or before THURSDAY the 2nd of APRIL next.

[3]
1 On what grounds did Macaulay, a Whig, support Wellington, a Tory, in opposing democracy? Explain their fears of universal suffrage.
2 Who were the new property owners whom Macaulay wanted to get into Parliament? Why would such people be opposed to increased taxation, revolution and greater democracy?
3 Name three cities which were *renowned*. Why were some of these not represented in Parliament?
4 The French middle classes had led the 1830 Revolution in France and the Bourbons had lost the throne. How did Macaulay apply this lesson to Britain?
5 Show the connection between the Industrial Revolution and Parliamentary Reform as regards (i) the franchise, and (ii) the distribution of constituencies.

[4]
1 Why did Mr Mangles provide so much free food for *his worthy Friends*? Why were men willing to spend money on elections?
2 How could Mr Mangles or his agent check on the way in which their *worthy Friends* voted? When was this made impossible?
3 Can you suggest how Mr Mangles's opponent might try to counter this appeal to the voters?
4 Compare Mr Mangles's appeal to the voter with a modern politician's. Can you see any similarities, and/or differences? Why would it be impossible for a candidate today to use Mr Mangles's tactics? When were such 'treaties' made illegal?

5 The passing of the first Reform Bill in the Commons, March 1831

[5]
1 Who introduced the Reform Bill in 1831? Who was Prime Minister at the time?
2 Why was it to be expected that the Bill would be defeated in the vote in the House of Commons?
3 What was the result of this vote in March 1831? Why did this Bill not go on to become an Act?
4 Why did the *jaw of Peel* fall? What office had he held under Wellington in 1830? What was his attitude towards Parliamentary Reform? When and how did he signify his acceptance of the principles of the Reform Act 1832?
5 How many Reform Bills came before the Commons in 1831–2? What happenened to the Second Reform Bill?
6 How did King William IV help to get the final Bill through the House of Lords in 1832?

Such a scene as the division of last Tuesday, I never saw, and never expect to see again . . . the crowd overflowed the House in every part . . . we have six hundred and eight members present. The Ayes and Noes were like two volleys of cannon from opposite sides of a field of battle. When the opposition went out into the lobby . . . we spread ourselves over the benches on both sides of the House. When the doors were shut we began to speculate on our numbers. Everybody was desponding. We have lost it. We are only two hundred and eighty at the most. They are three hundred. As the tellers passed along our lowest row on the left hand side the interest was insupportable—two hundred and ninety-one,—two hundred and ninety-two—We were all standing up and stretching forward, telling with the tellers. At three hundred there was a short cry of joy—at three hundred and two another—suppressed however in a moment, for we did not know yet what the hostile force might be.

The doors were thrown open and in they came. Each of them, as he entered, brought some different report of their numbers. We were all breathless with anxiety, when Charles Wood, who stood near the door, jumped on a bench and cried out 'They are only three hundred and one.' We set up a shout that you might have heard to Charing Cross, waving our hats, stamping the floor, and clapping our hands. The tellers scarcely got through the floor. But you might have heard a pin drop as Duncannon read the numbers. Then again the shouts broke out, and many of us shed tears. And the jaw of Peel fell, and the face of Twiss was as the face of a damned soul; and Herries looked like Judas taking his necktie off for the final operation.

(T. B. Macaulay in a letter, 3 March 1831)

6 The £10 householder

To the Right Hon. Lord John Russell.
Leeds Mercury Office, November 7th, 1831.

My Lord,

I am honoured by your Lordship's letter of the 3rd inst., asking if I possess any information concerning the numbers and respectability of the £10 householders in Leeds.

To enable me to give this information I convened a meeting of the principal Reformers in Leeds, who a few weeks ago canvassed the borough in favour of the two Liberal Candidates.

The following questions were put to the canvassers individually:-

1st. Does the result of your canvass lead you to conclude that the limitation of the franchise to householders renting £10 houses admits any considerable number of persons not fitted to vote for members?

2nd. Does the £10 qualification *exclude* any considerable number of persons suitable to vote?

3rd. Does the stipulation with respect to payment of rates and taxes exclude any considerable number of £10 householders?

4th. What is the proportion which the £10 householders bear to the population of the district?

The canvassers stated *unanimously*, that the £10 qualification did not admit a single person who might not safely be enfranchised.

To the second question they replied that the £10 qualification *did exclude* a great number who might be entrusted with the franchise.

The third question caused some difference of opinion. In some quarters of the town the landlord pays the rates and taxes for houses as high as £15 or £20 rent. Thus a very considerable number of respectable tenants would be deprived of a vote.

The answers to the fourth question varied according as the different divisions of the town were occupied principally by the working classes or by tradespeople. In the parts occupied chiefly by the working classes, not one householder in fifty would have a vote. In the streets principally occupied by shops, almost every householder had a vote. In the township of Holbeck, containing 11,000 inhabitants, chiefly of the working classes, but containing several mills, dye-houses, public-houses, and respectable dwellings, there are only 150 voters. If the qualification was raised to £15 house-rent, there would only be about 50 voters. Out of 140 householders, heads of families, working in the mill of Messrs. Marshall and Co., there are only two who will have votes. It appeared that of the working classes not more than one in fifty would be enfranchised by the Bill.

There will be in Leeds, the population of which is 124,000, the number of 6,683 voters. Making the deductions for female householders and uninhabited houses, and persons disqualified by the obligation to pay rates and taxes, the number of voters will be reduced to less than 5,000.

The general opinion of the canvassers was that the £10 qualification was rather too high than too low.

Your Lordship's most obedient humble servant,

Edward Baines.

[6]

1 Who were qualified to vote in borough elections after 1832? What changes did the 1832 Act make in the qualifications for the franchise in county elections?

2 Why did the Whigs fix the borough qualification at such a high level? What percentage of the population of Leeds might have been qualified to vote after 1832?

3 What was the significance of the answer to the second question asked by the canvassers in Leeds?

4 How were some *respectable tenants* excluded from qualifying for the franchise?

5 Why was there a high proportion of voters in some streets and a lower proportion in other streets?

6 Why did Baines have to make a deduction for female householders? Why were such deductions affected by Acts passed in (i) 1918, and (ii) 1928?

7 The Parliamentary system, 1831–1832

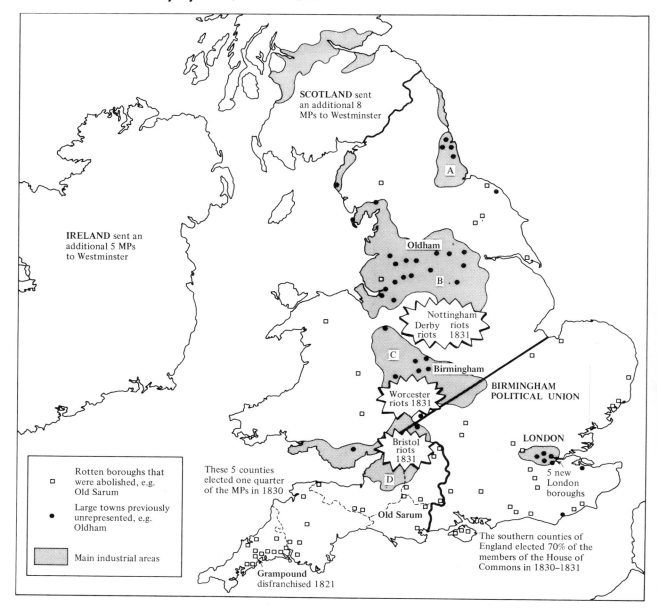

SCOTLAND sent an additional 8 MPs to Westminster

IRELAND sent an additional 5 MPs to Westminster

Oldham

A

B

Nottingham Derby riots 1831

C

Birmingham

BIRMINGHAM POLITICAL UNION

Worcester riots 1831

Bristol riots 1831

D

LONDON

5 new London boroughs

These 5 counties elected one quarter of the MPs in 1830

☐ Rotten boroughs that were abolished, e.g. Old Sarum

● Large towns previously unrepresented, e.g. Oldham

▨ Main industrial areas

Old Sarum

The southern counties of England elected 70% of the members of the House of Commons in 1830–1831

Grampound disfranchised 1821

[7] 1 Name two of the major industries which flourished in each of the areas marked A, B, C and D.

2 Which county in the south-west lost many rotten boroughs? Which county in the north-west contained towns which were first represented in Parliament because of the 1832 Act?

3 How many seats were redistributed by the 1832 Act? What does this tell you about the political power of southern England after 1832?

4 Why are the following towns marked on the sketch-map of the 1832 Act: Derby, Nottingham, Birmingham, Bristol, Grampound?

5 How did Wales, Ireland and Scotland benefit from the redistribution of seats in 1832?

8 Bath and Reform

On Wednesday the election for this city came on, when Lord John Thynne and Lieut.-Col. Palmer were re-elected by the Mayor, 10 Aldermen and 20 Common Council.

During the election Mr. Allen appeared in the Hall, and demanded a poll for himself and S. Graves Esq., insisting upon the right of the 110 Freemen of the City at large to vote. But they ignored him and carried on chairing the two Members. Mr. Allen, left in the Hall, then took the votes of several Freemen, and after three hours, had got 28 names in support of his claim.

(*The Bath Herald*, October 1812)

An analysis of the first reformed Parliament:

Bath: Population 38,063; number of £10 houses 7,314; the old constituency 33.

Bath has hitherto provided one of the most striking illustrations of the anomalies and corrupt absurdities of our constitution. Through a long course of years for ten Parliaments, we find Lord John Thynne, brother of the Marquis of Bath, voting against Reform, against Catholic Emancipation, against the Queen, and against every enlightened and patriotic measure.

(*The Weekly Dispatch*, January 1833)

9 Wellington to Croker, March 1833

I will endeavour to obtain for you the details regarding the state of the representation in the House of Commons. I have compared notes with others, and I think that all agree in the same story. The revolution is made; power is transferred from one class of society, the gentlemen of England, professing the faith of the Church of England, to another class of society, the shopkeepers, being dissenters from the Church.

I don't think that the influence of property in this country is diminished. That is to say, that the gentry have as many followers and influence as many voters at elections as ever they did.

But a new democratic influence has been introduced into elections, the copy-holders and free-holders and lease-holders residing in towns which do not themselves return members to Parliament. These are all dissenters from the Church, and are everywhere a formidably active party against the aristocratic influence of the Landed Gentry. But this is not all. There are dissenters in every village in the country; they are the black-smith, the carpenter, the mason, &c. &c. The new influence established in the towns has drawn these to their party; and it is curious to see to what a degree it is a dissenting interest. The mischief of the reform is that whereas democracy prevailed heretofore only in some places, it now prevails everywhere. There is no place exempt from it. In the great majority it is preponderant.

Believe me ever yours most sincerely,

Wellington

[8]
1 How many people wanted to claim the right to elect MPs in Bath in 1812? What qualification did they have for the franchise?
2 How many people actually elected the MPs in Bath in 1812? What positions did they hold in the city?
3 Which Party had the MPs from Bath supported between 1812 and 1832? Give two reasons for your answer.
4 What was the maximum number of people who might have voted in Bath in 1833? Why was the number qualifying to vote less than this maximum?
5 What percentage of people in Bath voted (i) in 1812, and (ii) in 1832?
6 What was the significance of *Catholic Emancipation* in (i) the resignation of Peel from Canning's Government, (ii) the resignation of Huskisson from Wellington's Government, and (iii) the fall of the Wellington Government in 1830?

[9]
1 What did Wellington think had happened to the nature of Parliament as regards (i) class, and (ii) religion?
2 How had *the influence of property* and *the gentry* been diminished by the 1832 Act? Do you agree with Wellington's views on this? Why?
3 Explain *copy-holders* and *lease-holders*.
4 Do you agree that *democracy . . . now prevails everywhere*? Why?

Topic 3 The Whigs, 1833–1841

1 Sheffield, a new town, 1831

Unlike many other large towns Sheffield cannot boast of its mayor and corporations. The power of the company of cutlers extends only to their own body, and until 1818 Sheffield had no advantage over the smallest town in the kingdom. In that year an Act was passed for the better regulation of the town under the title of 'an Act for cleansing, lighting, watching and otherwise improving the town of Sheffield.' The Act has been productive of considerable benefit to the town, but much remains yet to which its operation may be extended.

Commissioners were appointed to carry the Act into effect; their officers consist of a treasurer, clerk, surveyor and collector. The surveyor causes all offenders against the Act to appear before the magistrates, who sit at the town-hall every Tuesday and Friday, by whom they are examined and judged accordingly. . .

The Gas works are situated near Sheaf Bridge, and the building is highly ornamental. This company was formed about 1818, and the capital raised was £40,000 in shares of £25 each. An Act of Parliament was obtained and the company incorporated by the title of the 'Sheffield Gaslight Company'. The town was first lighted on the 6th October 1819.

The Water works are situated on Crook's moor, and were established in 1782. The Earl of Surrey, the Lord of the Manor at that time, granted the company a lease of the privileges they had enjoyed, in a smaller concern, of the kind, for ninety-nine years, the rent to be one-tenth of the profits of the company.

The principal reservoir is spread over four acres of land, and is calculated to contain, when full, three hundred thousand hogsheads. The water is conveyed to the working dam at Portbello, a distance of one thousand, one hundred yards, and from thence to a stone cistern in Division Street, containing about seven hundred hogsheads. From this reservoir it is carried by pipes to all parts of the town.

(T. Allen, *A New and Complete History of the County of York*, 1831)

[1]
1 Why did Sheffield not have a mayor and corporation? What does this tell you about the growth of the town?
2 Explain *cutlers*; *watching*; *magistrates*.
3 From whom and how did the improvement commissioners get the money they needed? How did they spend this money?
4 What was gas used for in the early nineteenth century? Who had first shown how it might be used for this purpose?
5 Who made a profit out of the water company? Why did many towns not have a supply of fresh water at this time?
6 How did Sheffield benefit from a clause in the Municipal Corporations Act, 1835?

2 The environment and health, 1842

1. The various forms of epidemic, endemic and other disease are caused chiefly amongst the labouring classes by atmospheric impurities produced by decomposing animal and vegetable substances, by damp and filth, and close and overcrowded dwellings.

2. Such disease, wherever its attacks are frequent, is always found in connexion with the physical circumstances above specified, and that where those circumstances are removed by drainage, proper cleansing, better ventilation and other means of diminishing atmospheric impurity, the frequency and intensity of such disease is abated.

3. That the formation of all habits of cleanliness is obstructed by defective supplies of water.

4. The most important measures, and at the same time the most practicable, are drainage, the removal of all refuse of habitations, streets and roads, and the improvement of the supplies of water.

5. By the combinations of all these arrangements, it is probable that the full ensurable period of life . . . that is, an increase of 13 years at least, may be extended to the whole of the labouring classes.

(Report from the Poor Law Commissioners of an inquiry into the sanitary conditions of the labouring population of Great Britain, 1842)

[2]

1 Why were the *Poor Law Commissioners* concerned about sanitary conditions?
2 Explain *epidemic, endemic.* Give one example of each type of disease which affected the British people in the early nineteenth century.
3 What *physical circumstances* helped the spread of disease?
4 Why did some people write about 'preventable' disease?
5 Why did the Commissioners want an increase in spending by councils and Improvement Commissioners? Why was this opposed by many influential people?
6 Why could these policies only be applied after the introduction of a system of efficient local government?

3 Cholera notice, 1832

4 Happy Hampstead, 1875

"HAPPY HAMPSTEAD!"
(A SUBURBAN PLAY(GUE) GROUND.)
Sunday-Outer. "HA, MY DEAR! NOW THIS IS WHAT I CALL PLEASANT AND SALOOBRIOUS! DO THE YOUNG 'UNS NO END O' GOOD. LET'S GET ON TO THE 'EATH."

CHOLERA.
THE
DUDLEY BOARD OF HEALTH,
HEREBY GIVE NOTICE, THAT IN CONSEQUENCE OF THE
Church-yards at Dudley
Being so full, no one who has died of the CHOLERA will be permitted to be buried after *SUNDAY* next, (To-morrow) in either of the Burial Grounds of St. *Thomas's,* or St. *Edmund's,* in this Town.

All Persons who die from CHOLERA, must for the future be buried in the Church-yard at Netherton.

BOARD of HEALTH, DUDLEY.
September 1st, 1832.

[3, 4]

1 Why was a middle-class family in less immediate danger from cholera, fever or smallpox than a poor family?
2 Why did cholera and other diseases lead to an increase in Poor Rates?
3 List four ways in which the better-off came into daily contact with the poor.
4 In what ways, other than personal contact, might disease be spread from the poor to the better-off?
5 Why were some middle-class people anxious to provide a healthier environment for the poor? Why did some oppose this?

5 Manchester workers, 1832

The population employed in the cotton factories rises at five o'clock in the morning, works in the mills from six till eight o'clock, and returns home for half an hour or forty minutes to breakfast. This meal generally consists of tea or coffee, with a little bread. Oatmeal porridge is sometimes, but of late rarely used, and chiefly by the men; but the stimulus of tea is preferred, and especially by the women. The tea is almost always of a bad, and sometimes of a deleterious quality; the infusion is weak, and little or no milk is added. The operatives return to the mills and workshops until twelve o'clock, when an hour is allowed for dinner. Amongst those who obtain the lower rates of wages, this meal generally consists of boiled potatoes. The mess of potatoes is put into one large dish; melted lard and butter are poured upon them, and a few pieces of fried bacon are sometimes mingled with them, and but seldom a little meat. Those who obtain the better wages, or families whose aggregate income is larger, add a greater proportion of animal food to this meal, at least three times in the week; but the quantity consumed by the labouring population is not great. The family sits around the table and each rapidly appropriates his portion on a plate, or they all plunge their spoons into the dish, and with animal eagerness satisfy the cravings of their appetite. At the expiration of the hour, they are all again employed in the workshop or the mills, where they continue until seven o'clock or a later hour, when they generally again indulge in the use of tea, often mingled with spirits accompanied by a little bread. Oatmeal or potatoes are however taken by some a second time in the evening.

(J. P. Kay-Shuttleworth, *The Moral and Physical Condition of the Working Classes*, 1832)

Children eating at a trough

6 The working-class environment

In the centre of the street is a gutter into which potato parings . . . the dirty water from the washing of clothes and of the houses are all poured, and there they stagnate. In a direct line from Virginia Road to Shoreditch, a mile in extent, all the lanes, courts and alleys in the neighbourhood, pour their contents into the centre of the main street where they putrefy. Families live in the cellars and kitchens of these under-ground houses, dark and extremely damp.

(Report of the Poor Law Commissioners, 1838)

[5, 6]

1 How many hours did the cotton operatives work? Why did factory owners want them to work such long hours?

2 Why did workers have to live within walking distance of their places of work? What were (i) the advantages, and (ii) the disadvantages of this?

3 What were the main deficiencies in the diet outlined here? Why did many children (and adults) scavenge for food in pig troughs?

4 Why was it common for refuse to be thrown into the streets? Who might have forbidden this? What services would have to be provided to make the streets cleaner?

5 Why did so many people live *in the cellars*?

6 List four causes of the high death rate in the 1830s.

7 The new Poor Law, 1834

The most pressing of the evils are those connected with the relief of the able-bodied. Circumstances will occur in which an individual, by the failure of his means of subsistence, will be exposed to the danger of perishing. To refuse relief is repugnant; therefore, the occurrence of extreme necessity is prevented by alms-giving; and the public is warranted in imposing . . . conditions on the individual relieved.

The first is that his situation shall not be made as eligible as the situation of the independent labourer of the lowest class. When the condition of the pauper class is elevated above the condition of independent labourers these persons are under the strongest inducements to quit the less eligible class of labourers, and enter the more eligible class of paupers. We recommend . . . First, that except as to medical attendance . . . all relief to able-bodied persons or families otherwise than in well-regulated workhouses, shall be declared unlawful. We recommend the appointment of a Central Board to control the administration of the Poor Laws, with such Assistant Commissioners as may be found requisite; and that the Commissioners be empowered to enforce regulations for the government of workhouses, and the nature and amount of the relief to be given, and the labour to be exacted in them, and that such regulations shall be uniform throughout the country.

(Report of the Commissioners on the Poor Law, 1834)

[7]
1 What was the meaning of *able-bodied*? How had these been helped by the Poor Law authorities before 1834? Why was there no uniformity in the way in which the poor were treated before 1834?
2 What *circumstances* might cause someone to ask for relief?
3 Why did the *condition of the pauper* have to be made less *eligible* than that of the poorest paid workman? Why would that lead to a fall in the level of poor rates?
4 How were the able-bodied to get relief after 1834?
5 What was the main importance of the work of the Central Board?

8 The attack on the workhouse at Stockport

[8]
1 Explain the use of the word *Union* over the doorway.
2 Why did many people describe the *Workhouse* as a Bastille?
3 Who elected the people responsible for the way in which Workhouses were organised and run? Who, in turn, supervised these elected officers?
4 Why were attacks on the Workhouses more common in the north of England than in the south?

9 The Factory Act of 1833

No person under eighteen years of age shall [work] between half-past eight in the evening and half-past five in the morning, in any cotton, woollen, worsted, hemp, flax, tow, linen or silk mill. No person under the age of eighteen shall be employed in any such mill more than twelve hours in one day, nor more than sixty-nine hours in one week. There shall be allowed not less than one and a half hours for meals.

It shall not be lawful to employ in any factory as aforesaid except in mills for the manufacture of silk, any child who shall not have completed his or her ninth year. It shall not be lawful for any person to employ in any factory as aforesaid for longer than forty-eight hours in one week, nor for longer than nine hours in one day, any child who shall not have completed his or her eleventh year.

It shall be lawful for His Majesty to appoint four Inspectors of factories where children and young persons under eighteen years of age are employed. The Inspectors shall have power to make such rules as may be necessary for the execution of this Act, binding on all persons subject to the provisions of this Act.

Every child restricted to the performance of forty-eight hours of labour in any one week shall attend some school.

Children in the factories

[9] 1 To what factories did the 1833 Act apply? Where did children go to find work when they were forbidden to work in these factories?
2 Which children were forbidden to work in some factories after 1833? Why was it difficult to enforce this regulation until the Registration Act had been passed in 1837?
3 Which children were allowed to work a limited number of hours? What else did the 1833 Act say about these children?
4 What was the significance of the appointment of *four Inspectors*? Who had been responsible for enforcing previous Factory Acts? Why had their work been, generally, ineffective?

10 Getting and carrying the slaves

Mr. James Towne, Carpenter of His Majesty's Ship Syren, called in and examined:

Do you know anything of the mode by which slaves are obtained? The general way was that when a ship comes on the coast they generally send for the traders, and make them presents, to encourage them to bring any person to sell as a slave. The Black Kings have told me that they were going to war to get slaves, and I have seen their men prisoners brought in bound, the women and children loose, and immediately were delivered up to the white traders, or else drove down in gangs of two or three hundred to the water side for sale to the best bidder.

Were the Negroes fettered on board the ships which you have known? Always; with legshakels and handcuffs; two and two, right and left.

Has the space on board ship been sufficient for their convenience or health? By no means; they lay in a crowded and cramped state. I have known them to go down well, and in the morning brought up dead, from the suffocated state they were in down below.

Do you recollect the height between decks of the ships in which you sailed? The *Peggy* was about four feet.

(The Minutes of the Select Committee on the Slave Trade, 1791)

11 Gladstone opposes the abolition of slavery

As regards immediate emancipation, whether with or without compensation, there are several minor reasons against it; but that which weighs with me is that it would, I much fear, exchange the evils now affecting the negro for others which are weightier—for a relapse into deeper abasement, if not, for bloodshed and internal war. Let fitness be made a condition for emancipation; Let him enjoy the means of earning his freedom through honest and industrious habits; and thus, I earnestly trust, without risk of blood, without violation of property, with unimpaired benefit to the negro, and with the utmost speed which prudence will admit, we shall arrive at that exceedingly desirable consummation, the utter extinction of slavery.

(Gladstone, address to the electors of Newark, 1832)

12 The abolition of slavery, 1833

There can be no doubt that a great many of the Abolitionists are actuated by very pure motives; they have been shocked at the cruelties which have been and still are very often practised towards slaves, their minds are imbued with the horrors they have read and heard of, and they have an invincible conviction that the state of slavery under any form is repugnant to the spirit of the English Constitution and the Christian religion, and that it is a stain upon the national character which ought to be wiped away. These people, generally speaking, are very ignorant concerning all the various difficulties which beset the questions.

Talking over the matter the other day, Henry Taylor (of the Colonial Office) said that he was well aware of the consequences of emancipation both to the negroes and the planters. The estates of the latter would not be cultivated; it would be impossible, for want of labour; the negroes would not work—no inducement would be sufficient to make them; they wanted to be free merely that they might be idle. They would, on being emancipated, possess themselves of ground, the fertility of which in those regions is so great that very trifling labour will be sufficient to provide them with the means of existence, and they will thus relapse rapidly into a state of barbarism; they will resume the habits of their African brethren, but, he thinks, without the ferocity and savageness which distinguish the latter.

(*The Greville Memoirs*, 1852)

[10, 11, 12]

1 How did the native chiefs get the slaves to sell to the English? How did the English persuade them to sell their slaves?

2 Why did many slaves die on the journey from Africa to America? Why were they kept in *legshakels and handcuffs* while on board ship?

3 Explain *compensation*. How much was finally paid? Who considered this to be insufficient?

4 Explain the differences between Gladstone and the Abolitionists over the way in which emancipation should be achieved.

5 Why, according to Taylor, would former slaves not work after abolition? How far was this opinion based on good evidence? How far was it the expression of bias?

6 How did emancipation affect (i) West Indian sugar planters, and (ii) the Dutch settlers in South Africa?

Topic 4 Peel, 1841–1846

1 Peel and income tax, 1842

Instead of looking to taxation on consumption, it is my duty to make an appeal to the possessors of property, for the purpose of repairing this mighty evil. I propose that the income of this country should bear a charge not exceeding 7d in the pound; for the purpose of not only supplying the deficiency in the revenue, but of enabling me to propose great commercial reforms, which will afford a hope or reviving commerce, and, by diminishing the prices of the articles of consumption, and the cost of living, will compensate you for your present sacrifices. In 1798, the Minister had the courage to propose an income tax of 10 per cent. The income tax continued to the close of the war in 1802; and in 1803, after the rupture of the peace of Amiens, a duty of 5 per cent was placed upon property. It was raised in 1805 to 6¼ per cent; and so it continued to the end of the war. I propose that the duty to be laid on property shall not exceed 3 per cent, being 7d in the pound. Under the former tax, all incomes below £60 were exempt from taxation and on incomes between £60 and £150 the tax was reduced. I recommend all incomes under £150 shall be exempt.

(Peel's Budget Speech, 11 March 1842)

[1]
1 Why did *taxation on consumption* affect the poor more than the better-off?
2 Why did cuts in *taxation on consumption* lead to a fall in the cost of living? Why was this welcomed by British workers? Why was it welcomed by manufacturers of goods sold in the British home market?
3 Which Prime Minister had proposed an income tax in 1798? Why? When had this tax been abolished?
4 How did Peel's income tax differ from that of 1798?
5 How much income tax had to be paid by people earning (i) £200, (ii) £400, (iii) £600 a year?

2 Peel's Free Trade Budget, 1842

I calculate on a surplus of £1,800,000. In what way shall we apply it? I propose to apply it by improvements in the commercial tariff of England, and to abate the duties on some great articles of consumption. Sir, the tariff comprises not less than 1,200 articles subject to various rates of duty. We desire to remove all prohibition, and the relaxation of duties of a prohibitory character; next, we wish to reduce the duties on raw materials for manufactures to no more than 5 per cent. The duties on articles partly manufactured shall be materially reduced, never exceeding 12 per cent. As to duties on articles wholly manufactured we propose that they shall never exceed 20 per cent.

(Peel in the House of Commons, 25 April 1842)

[2]
1 What was the major difference in the outcome of the budgets of the previous Government and of Peel's budget of 1842?
2 How did Peel propose to use the budget surplus he hoped to get?
3 Who had reduced import duties in the 1820s?
4 What was the effect of the reduction in *duties on raw materials* on the prices of finished goods? Why was this welcomed by (i) British consumers, (ii) manufacturers engaged in the export trades?
5 Why did Peel's proposals help to increase the level of employment?
6 Why were some duties lower than the 5%, 12%, and 20% mentioned in the extract?

3 The effect of the railways

British railways were spreading, like a network, over Great Britain and Ireland, to the extent of 8,054 miles completed; thus, in length, they exceeded the ten chief rivers of Europe united and more than enough of single rails were laid to make a belt of iron round the globe. The cost of these lines had been £86,000,000. 80,000,000 train miles were run annually on the railways, 5,000 engines and 150,000 vehicles composed the working stock . . . the engines consumed annually 2,000,000 tons of coal, so that in every minute of time four tons of coal flashed into steam twenty tons of water. The coal consumed was equal to the whole amount exported to foreign countries . . . 20,000 tons of iron required to be replaced annually; and 26,000,000 sleepers annually perished. The postal facilities afforded by railways were very great. But for their existence Mr. Rowland Hill's plan could never have been effectually carried out. Railways afforded the means of carrying bulk, which would have been fatal to the old mail coaches. They were the great engines for the diffusion of knowledge. The results of railways were astounding. 90,000 men were employed directly and upwards of 40,000 collaterally; 130,000 men with their wives and families, representing a population of 500,000 souls; so that one in fifty of the entire population of the kingdom might be said to be dependent on railways.

(Robert Stephenson, address to the Institution of Civil Engineers, 1856)

[3]
1 What does this extract tell you about the Victorians' attitude towards their railways?
2 How did the growth of railways affect coal mining, iron making, civil engineering and mechanical engineering?
3 How did the railways affect the owners of canals and stage coaches?
4 What was *Mr. Rowland Hill's plan*? Why did it depend on the railway system?
5 What other forms of communication were affected by the growth of railways?
6 How did the railway system affect the people's diet, holidays and home?
7 How did the growth of a railway system affect the following towns: Crewe, Middlesborough, Grimsby, Cardiff and Bournemouth?

4 The Tring cutting

[4]
1 Explain the methods used to excavate the cutting shown here. Name two tasks being done by men which, today, would be done by machines.
2 From where did the building companies get their labourers? Why were they called *navvies*?
3 What various kinds of difficulties faced the railway engineers?
4 Name three of the most famous railway engineers of this period.
5 What was the importance of the work of George Hudson for the development of the railway network?

5 An attack on Peel, 1845

There is no question which he has handled, on which he has not run us aground. What can we say of our future voyage, when in past times our pilot has so failed us?

His course has always been the same. He fancies that he looks ahead; the truth is, that he sticks to his course till the soundings tell him that he is on the sands, then, in haste and alarm, he throws his cargo in one moment overboard. He took this course on Emancipation. He was the champion of the Protestants; No surrender, was his cry. Then on a sudden loomed the breakers, the Clare election; the terror of an Irish rebellion. Instantly, helm about, and the whole cargo, the professions of a life, were cleared at a blow. So it was on Reform; not a point would he concede, not a member to Birmingham, not a representative to Manchester; then, defeated, he made a total change, every principle recast and turned upside down to suit, as he thinks, a new world.

Look, lastly, at his conduct on the Corn-laws . . . at first, agricultural protection was essential to land, to labour and to trade. This doctrine he preached from 1815 to 1830, earnestly and loudly. In 1837 he was its advocate; he fought the fight in 1838, 1839 and 1840; he clenched it, as we have shown, in 1841. Is he the advocate of protection still? Read the speeches which he and Sir James Graham delivered on 10th of June last. What do they all say of Sir Robert Peel's views of protection? That they are gone, that the game is up; that protective duties are to be abandoned. All his arguments that protection was essential to the farmer; that it was needful to be independent of foreign supply; these statements made, dwelt upon, repeated with the dexterity of a first rate debater and the authority of a party leader, enforced with the utmost seriousness, as if he really felt and believed them, are gone, absolutely gone!

(J. C. Colquhoun MP, 'The Effects of Sir Robert Peel's Administration', in *The English Review*, December 1845)

[5]
1 List the three *questions* on which *he has . . . run us aground*.
2 What was the significance of *the Clare election*? What office did Peel hold at the time? What Act had he piloted through the Commons as a result of that Election?
3 When and how had he signified his *total change* towards Reform?
4 What arguments had Peel used in defence of the Corn Laws?
5 Which Tory MP made similar speeches attacking Peel in 1845 and 1846?
6 Do you think that it is a sign of weakness or of strength for a party leader to be willing to change his mind? Why?

6 Samuel Smiles on self-help, 1859

'Heaven helps those who help themselves' is a well-tried maxim. The spirit of self-help is the root of all genuine growth in the individual, and it constitutes the true source of national vigour and strength. Whatever is done *for* men or classes takes away the necessity for doing for themselves, and where men are subjected to over-government, the tendency is to render them comparatively helpless.

Mr. Bright observed in 1847, 'There is only one way by which men can maintain their present position if it be a good one, or raise themselves above it if it be a bad one,—that is, by the practice of the virtues of industry, frugality, temperance and honesty. What has made the middle class, but these virtues? There was a time when there was hardly any class in England, except the highest. How is it that hundreds of thousands of men of the middle class, are educated, comfortable, and enjoying an amount of happiness and independence, to which our forefathers were wholly unaccustomed? Why, by the practice of

[6]
1 How does this extract help to explain early Victorian attitudes towards (i) factory reform, (ii) public health, and (iii) the Poor Law?
2 How did *the spirit of self-help* promote Britain's economic development?
3 What undesirable results followed from a policy of self-help?
4 What part did Bright play in (i) the campaign against the Corn Laws, (ii) factory reform?
5 How did some working class men practise self-help in (i) trade unions, (ii) building societies? Why was this possible only for a minority of working men?

those very virtues. I would recommend every man to pay no attention whatever to writers or speakers who tell them that this class or that class, that this law or that law, that this Government or that Government, can do all these things for them. There is no way for the working classes of this country to improve their condition, but by the practice of those virtues, and by reliance upon themselves.'

(Samuel Smiles, *Self-Help*, 1859)

7 The first co-operative, 1844

The objects of this Society are to form arrangements for the pecuniary benefit and improvement of the social and domestic condition of its members, by raising capital in shares of one pound each, to bring into operation the following plans.

The establishment of a store for the sale of provisions, clothing, etc.

The purchasing or erecting of a number of houses, in which those members desiring to assist each other in improving their domestic and social conditions may reside.

To commence the manufacture of such articles as the Society may determine upon, for the employment of such members as may be without employment or who may be suffering in consequence of repeated reduction in their wages.

(Rules of the Rochdale Society of Equitable Pioneers, 1844)

8 Founding a co-operative shop in Cramlington, 1865

The members held meetings and subscribed about £20. Two were sent to Newcastle to make the first purchases. They laid out the money to the best of their ability, buying a cask of herrings, a side of bacon, a firkin of butter, coffee, tea, sugar, tobacco, etc., and not omitting lucifer matches into which they went largely. Their return was looked for anxiously. At last a little spring cart made its appearance, which caused some to come out and stand laughing at the madcaps. The cart having got to the little room, the shop was opened. The stock was nearly sold out, except the matches, on the first Friday night and the two men went to buy more. They went on this way for the first three months, doubling and trebling their orders, till at last the dividend was declared. The number of members now rapidly increased. Men who had been fettered to a shop by the credit system all their lives began to look for themselves. Ladies, instead of running up ruinous accounts at ordinary shops became energetic supporters of the new movement. In the first quarter £450 was received, realising a profit of £39. The receipts for the quarter ending March 1873 amounted to £23,000 of which £2,478 was profit. The members had increased from 80 to 1688.

(R. Fynes, *Miners of Northumberland and Durham*, 1923)

[7, 8]
1 Why did the *Rochdale Pioneers* start their co-operative? How far was this an example of self-help?
2 How did they hope to affect their *domestic and social condition*?
3 How did the aims of the Rochdale Pioneers differ from those of the founders of the co-operative at Cramlington?
4 How did working men raise the capital they needed to start a co-operative? Why could most working men not afford to become members?
5 When and why was there an increase in the number of members in the Cramlington co-operative? What good habits had this co-operative encouraged?
6 Why was the growth of the co-operative movement opposed by existing shopkeepers?

9 Chadwick on life and death, 1842

Mr. Baker, in his report on the condition of the population, after giving an instance of the contrast presented by the working people living in better dwellings, describes the population living in houses—'With broken panes in every window frame, and filth and vermin in every nook. With walls unwhitewashed for years, black with the smoke of foul chimneys, without water, with corded bed-stocks for beds, and sacking for bed-clothing, with floors unwashed from year to year, without out-offices . . . while without there are streets, elevated a foot, sometimes two, above the level of the causeway, by the accumulation of years, and stagnant puddles here and there, with their foetid exhalations, causeways broken and dangerous, ash-places choked up with filth . . . undrained, unpaved, unventilated, uncared-for by any authority but the landlord, who weekly collects his miserable rents from his miserable tenants.'

Comparative Chances of Life, Average Age of Death

	In Manchester (Years)	In Rutlandshire (Years)
Professional persons and gentry, and their families:	38	52
Tradesmen and their families, (in Rutlandshire farmers are included):	20	41
Mechanics, labourers and their families:	17	38

(Edwin Chadwick, from the report on the sanitary conditions of the labouring population, 1842)

[9]

1 Why were some working class people forced to live in such conditions?

2 Why were some working people able to live in better conditions? How far was this due to their own self-help?

3 Why was there a higher rate of unemployment and poverty in (i) 1838–42, and (ii) 1847–9, than in other years in the 1830s and 1840s? Which political movement grew during these years?

4 Explain the significance of the varying death rates (i) in Manchester, and (ii) between Manchester and Rutlandshire. How were such figures used by sanitary reformers?

A cellar dwelling

10 Children in the mines

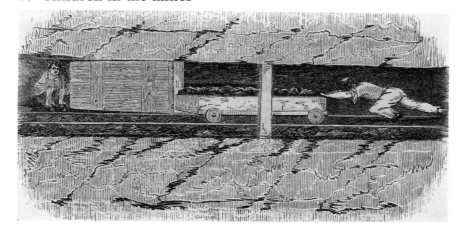

Trapper boy

(a) The evidence of Mr. Wild, Chief Constable of Oldham:
There is a class of accidents of which children employed at coalworks are the cause. These occur in the winding up by the steam-machinery of all persons out of the pit. It is a general system to employ children to stop these engines at the proper moment. If they be not stopped, the persons wound up together are thrown over the beam down into the pit again. The inducement to employ children in circumstances where life and death depend on their attention, is that their services can be obtained for perhaps 5s. or 7s. a week instead of the 30s. a week which the proprietors would have to pay a man. Three or four boys were killed in this way at the Chamberlane Colliery of Messrs. Jones by the neglect of a little boy only nine years of age who had turned away from the engine when it was winding up, his attention being distracted by a mouse in the hearth.

(Report of Commissioners on Children's Employment, 1842)

(b) A report
The hurriers, who haul the coal, buckle round their naked persons a broad leather strap, to which is attached in front a ring and about 4 feet of chain ending in a hook. As soon as they enter the main gates they detach their harness, change their position by getting behind it, and become 'thrusters'. The vehicle is then placed upon the rail, a candle is stuck fast by a piece of wet clay, and away they run, pushing their load with their heads and hands. The command they hold over it at every curve and angle, considering the pace, the unevenness of the floors and rails, and the mud, water and stones, is truly astonishing. I know few gates that will allow the use of horses; hence has arisen the substitution of children. In the Booth Town Pit I walked, crept and rode 1,800 yards to one of the nearest faces; the most distant was 200 yards further; the floor of the gate was inches deep in water, and muddy throughout. The roofs and walls are sometimes even, at others rough, rocky and loose, requiring proppings to prevent their falling; despite, however, the utmost precautions, large masses occasionally fall.

(Royal Commission on Mines, 1842)

[10]
1 Why did mines have to have doors like the one shown in the picture? How would opening the door affect the flow of fresh air into the mine?
2 Why was the trapper's job more lonely than that of the boys and girls who worked in other parts of the mine? Why would it be even more frightening if the candle was blown out?
3 What job was done by children at pit heads? Why did mine owners use child labour and not adult workers? What dangers were there from employing children?
4 What three different ways of transporting coal underground are mentioned? Why was child labour preferred to the use of animals?
5 Why did more children seek work at coal-mines after the passing of the Factory Act of 1833?
6 Why did the coal industry expand in the 1830s and 1840s?
7 Why were many children injured while working in coal-mines? What was the effect of such work on the health of children who were not injured?
8 What were the main effects of the Mines Act 1842 on employment in the coal industry?

Topic 5 Chartism and the Anti-Corn Law League

1 Depression

(a) 1843

Some idea may be formed of the extent to which the iron trade of South Staffordshire is depressed, by the fact that out of 111 blast furnaces fifty-three are blown out and are wholly unproductive either of labour or interest on the large capital expended on their erection. Some have been out more than a year; on an average the whole number has been out at least that period, and as they would each produce full eighty tons of iron per week, the quantity withdrawn from the market is, at the lowest calculation, 220,480 tons, and yet, with this immense reduction in the make, the market is still overstocked, prices are receding, wages are being still further reduced, and the capital necessary to the advantageous carrying on of the operations involved in the manufacture of iron, is being irrecoverably lost; while the sufferings of those usually employed at the iron works are, from want of employ, on the increase.

(*The Sunday Times*, 30 April 1843)

(b) 1847

Perhaps at no period within the remembrance of the oldest inhabitant have distress and privation pressed more heavily on the working classes than at the present moment. The streets are crowded with paupers, most of them Irish, who have travelled to Manchester from Liverpool, in the hope either of obtaining employment, or sharing with others from the public bounty of the town. A soup kitchen has been established, from which are distributed daily some 6,000 quarts of nutritious soup, with 1,000 loaves of bread. It is remarkable that of the recipients of this charity nine-tenths are Irish people. The operative classes employed in mills and manufactories (most of whom are working short time) seem to shrink from an application for charity, and prefer existence on the limited means derived from their labour. In the midst of so much want and misery it is gratifying to observe that not the slightest evidence of insubordination has shown itself. The working people generally seem to be of the opinion that the distress from which they are now suffering has proceeded from no causes over which the Government has had control.

(*The Times*, 17 February 1847)

[1]

1 What percentage of blast furnaces were not at work in South Staffordshire? Why was there a falling demand for iron at this time?

2 Why did this depression in the Staffordshire iron industry indicate that unemployment was also high in (i) South Wales, and (ii) north-east England?

3 Why was there a sharp fall in many people's living standards in 1842? What adjective is often used to describe the 1840s?

4 During 1844–5 there took place what has been described as 'the railway mania'. What effect did this have on the level of activity in the iron industry? Why was this industry depressed once again in 1847?

5 Why were there so many Irish paupers in Liverpool in 1847? How did their presence affect wage rates and unemployment levels?

6 Why was there so much *short time* working in cotton mills? What effect did this have on people's living standards? Why did it lead to a falling demand for non-cotton goods?

7 Why did the people not blame the Government? How did this attitude affect their attitudes towards Chartism?

2 The Corn Laws and emigration (by a Chartist)

Because our lords have taxed the staff of life,
The working man, his children, and his wife
All slave together, yet they must not eat—
Toil gives an appetite, but brings no meat!
The price of bread by law is kept so high,
That what we earn suffices not to buy,
But, why is this? What makes our bread so dear?
Far cheaper 'tis abroad than it is here!
Yes, but a tax is laid on foreign grain,
To make our home-grown corn its price maintain;
And half-fed men may toil, and starve, and die,
That idle lords may lift their heads on high.
We might buy cheap, but landlords want great rents,
To spend in keeping grand establishments.
The tenant says, if corn comes duty free,
'Twill bring down prices here, and ruin me;
Taxes and rents in England are so high,
I cannot sell so cheap as you could buy.
The honest husbandman must emigrate,
And leave poor peasants to increase the rate,
Unless our lords consent to live on less,
And pride succumb to humble happiness!

(John Watkins, *The Northern Star*, 1 January 1842)

[2]
1 Which law kept the *price of bread . . . so high*? Did the repeal of that law lead to the expected sharp fall in bread prices? Why?
2 Who benefited from the high prices of corn? How did they gain that benefit and how did they spend the higher incomes it earned them?
3 What part was played by the tenants in the arguments over prices and rents?
4 Why did millions of people emigrate from Victorian Britain? Name four countries to which they went.
5 Which *rate* would increase during a trade depression? Why?

3 The beginnings of the Anti-Corn Law League

On the 10th January 1839 a meeting was held at the York Hotel 'to consider the proper mode of carrying forward the proceedings of the Anti-Corn Law Association in a manner commensurate with the magnitude of the obstacles to be surmounted.' Mr. Cobden recommended to those present an investment of part of their property, and subscriptions were at once put down in the room for £1,800 and in the course of a month they had reached £6,136.10s.0d. These proceedings gave vitality to the Association which was soon enlarged and adopted the title of 'The National Anti-Corn Law League'. A small room in Newall's buildings, Market Street, was hired for our meetings, and when first opened there were usually not more than seven or eight members present. When it became publicly known that an Association was in existence having in view the repeal of the Corn Law, people came from far and near, giving most doleful accounts of mills and other works which were standing idle, whilst the operatives were dependent on charity or on their various parishes for support. The Association had no funds to relieve this distress, and could only advance the object of the distressed by the publication of properly authenticated statements in the newspapers.

These statements brought the League into notice, and led to many small donations of money to advance its usefulness.

(Henry Ashworth, *Recollections of Richard Cobden MP and the Anti-Corn Law League*, 1877)

[3]
1 Show the difference between Chartism and the Anti-Corn Law League as regards (i) the social class of their leaders, (ii) the income available to both organisations, (iii) the nature of the objectives of the two organisations. How far do these answers help to explain the success of one and failure of the other organisation?
2 Why did the League need an income? Give four ways in which this would be spent.
3 Which newspapers supported (i) the League, (ii) Chartism?

NO FOOD TAX!

The direct loss to the country by the Food Taxes is upwards of Fifty Millions sterling a year!

The Landlords' Tax on every Dozen of Flour averages nearly Tenpence!! And this is not for the State Revenue, but exclusively for their OWN BENEFIT!!!

ELECTORS OF WALSALL!

THINK OF THIS, AND

Vote for Smith

AND THE

REPEAL OF THE CORN LAWS.

5 Free Trade and the Corn Laws

From the middle of 1842 free trade measures have been in operation with evidence of the increasing ease and comfort of the people. Other causes have contributed; but even if the whole effect be assigned to those other causes, to railway enterprise, or anything else, it does not affect my present argument.

It was from diminished confidence in the advantage of protection—from the difficulty of resisting the application to food of those principles which had been applied to so many other articles—from the evidence of rapidly increasing consumption—from the aggravation of every other difficulty in the maintenance of the Corn Laws, by the fact of their suspension on the first real pressure—it was from the combined influence of such considerations that I came to the conclusion that the attempt to maintain those laws would be impolitic.

(Sir Robert Peel, letter to the electors of Tamworth, 1847)

6 Cobden on the Corn Laws

We want free trade in Corn, because we think it just. We do not seek free trade in corn for the purpose of purchasing it at a cheaper money rate, we require it at the natural price of the world's market. Whether it becomes dearer with a free trade—or whether it is cheaper, it matters not to us, provided the people have it at its natural price, and every source of supply is freely opened. We do not believe that free trade in corn will injure the farmer, we are convinced that it will benefit the tenant-farmer as much as any trader or manufacturer in the community.

Neither do we believe it will injure the farm labourer; we think it will enlarge the market for his labour. There will also be a general rise in

[4]
1 How, according to this poster, would Repeal affect landowners?
2 What was the more common name for the *Food Tax*?
3 How had the 1832 Reform Act (i) helped the Repealers, and (ii) disappointed the Chartists? Why was the League better able to mount a campaign *inside* Parliament?
4 How did the officials of the League ensure that (i) the electors were informed about their campaign, and (ii) they used their vote?
5 Explain how the League's campaign was helped by (i) the railway network, and (ii) the Penny Post.
6 Why would Repeal lead to increased imports and exports?

[5]
1 Why did Peel refer to *the middle of 1842*? What *free trade measures* had he introduced in that year?
2 How had free trade brought an *increasing ease and comfort of the people*? Why would (i) the Chartists, (ii) many industrial workers, and (iii) many agricultural workers have disagreed with that verdict?
3 How had railways helped to bring *ease and comfort* to people?
4 What connection did Peel see between his budgets of 1842 and 1845 and the arguments against the Corn Laws? Which leading Tory MP did not agree with him?
5 What was *the first real pressure* which led to the suspension of the Corn Laws?

wages from the increased demand for employment in the neighbouring towns, which will give young peasants an opportunity of choosing between the labour of the field and that of the towns.

We believe that free trade will increase the demand for labour of every kind, for the mechanical classes and those engaged in laborious bodily occupations, for clerks, shopmen and warehousemen. Finally we believe that Free Trade will not diminish but, on the contrary, increase the Queen's revenue.

(Speech in London, 3 July 1844)

7 Peel's cheap bread shop

PEEL'S CHEAP BREAD SHOP,
OPENED JANUARY 22, 1846.

[6]

1 How far, if at all, was there *free trade* in 1844?
2 What happened to the price of bread in the 1850s?
3 Why did free trade in corn lead to benefit for (i) the tenant–farmer, (ii) the farm labourer?
4 When did free trade in corn *injure the farmer*? Why?
5 Why were farmers forced to undertake improvements after 1846?
6 Why was there an *increased demand for employment* in manufacturing towns after 1846?
7 Which of *the Queen's revenues* might be expected to fall if there was Free Trade? Which might have been expected to rise?

[7]

1 What was the name of the political party led by *Russell*?
2 Why might *Russell* and his party have been expected to support Peel's policy in 1846?
3 What was the name of the political party led by *Peel*?
4 Why might that party have been expected to oppose the policy of *Cheap Bread*?
5 What happened to the price of bread in the 1850s? How do you explain the fact that there was no *Great Fall*? When did such a *Fall* occur?

8 William Lovett on Chartism, 1839

The General convention of the Industrious Classes originated with the Birmingham Political Union as did also . . . the first National Petition. The Delegates to this body were appointed by very large bodies of men. The Birmingham meeting was composed of 200,000; the Manchester meeting of 300,000; that of Glasgow, 150,000 . . . and other towns equally large in proportion to their population. The number of delegates composing the Convention was fifty-three. There were three magistrates, six newspaper editors, one clergyman of the Church of England, one Dissenting Minister and two doctors . . . the remainder being shopkeepers, tradesmen and journeymen. They held their first meeting at the British Coffee House, Cockspur Street, on February 4th 1839.

(William Lovett, *Life and Struggle*, 1876)

9 Chartism and physical force

I am for a strong police, but the people should have universal suffrage, the ballot, annual Parliaments and systematic education. England has an abundance of bad laws, but is every man to arm against every law he thinks bad? No! But laws must be reformed by the concentrated reason of the nation gradually acting on the legislature, not by pikes of individuals acting on the bodies of the executive.

The Chartists say that they will keep the sacred month [the national strike]. Folly! They will do no such thing; the poor cannot do it; they must plunder and then they will be hanged by the hundreds. Physical force! Fools! We have the physical force, not they. They talk of their hundreds of thousands of men. Who is to move them when I am dancing round them with cavalry?

(*Life and Opinions of General Sir Charles Napier*, 1857)

10 Chartism—a revolution?

April 6, 1848. I saw the Duke in the morning at Apsley House in a prodigious state of excitement, said he had plenty of troops, and would answer for keeping everything quiet if the Government would only be firm and vigorous, and announce by a proclamation that the mob should not be permitted to occupy the town. He wanted to prevent groups from going into the Park and assembling there, but this would be impossible.

April 9, 1848. All London is making preparation to encounter a Chartist row tomorrow. All the clerks are ordered to be sworn in special constables, and to constitute themselves into garrisons. I went to the police office with all my clerks, messengers, etc., and we were all sworn. We are to pass the whole day at the office tomorrow, and I am to send down all my guns. Colonel Harness of the Railway Department is our Commander in Chief; every gentleman in London is become a constable, and there is an organisation of some sort in every district.

[8, 9]

1 Who had formed *the Birmingham Political Union*? Why? What link was there between the origins of that Union and the aims of the Chartists?
2 Why was there no mention of a manufacturer or industrialist among the delegates? Why did they not support Chartism? What was the value of the support they gave to the Anti-Corn Law League?
3 Who led the *physical force* party? Why did this group frighten many people who might have been sympathetic to Chartism?
4 Why, according to Napier, could physical force never succeed? How might one of those who advocated physical force have defended their policies?
5 Why did *the sacred month* not win much support among working people in (i) 1839, (ii) 1843, (iii) 1847?

[10]

1 Explain (i) *the Duke*, (ii) *the Park*.
2 What did the Government fear might happen in London in April 1848? How far were their fears justified? What preparations did the Government make?
3 Where did the Chartists gather outside London? How did the Government prevent their marching on the House of Commons?
4 Which Chartists were *going northwards* along Whitehall?

April 13, 1848. Monday passed off with surprising quiet, and it was considered a most satisfactory demonstration on the part of the Government, and the peaceable and loyal part of the community. The Chartist movement was contemptible.

In the morning (a very fine day) everybody was on the alert; the parks were closed; our office was fortified, a barricade of Council Registers was erected in the accessible room on the ground floor, and all our guns were taken down to be used in defence of the building. However, at about twelve o'clock crowds came streaming along Whitehall, going northward, and it was announced that all was over. The intended tragedy was rapidly changed into a ludicrous farce.

(*The Greville Memoirs*, 1852)

11 The six points of the Charter

The Six Points
OF THE
PEOPLE'S
CHARTER.

1. A VOTE for every man twenty-one years of age, of sound mind, and not undergoing punishment for crime.

2. THE BALLOT.—To protect the elector in the exercise of his vote.

3. No PROPERTY QUALIFICATION for Members of Parliament —thus enabling the constituencies to return the man of their choice, be he rich or poor.

4. PAYMENT OF MEMBERS, thus enabling an honest tradesman, working man, or other person, to serve a constituency, when taken from his business to attend to the interests of the country.

5. EQUAL CONSTITUENCIES, securing the same amount of representation for the same number of electors, instead of allowing small constituencies to swamp the votes of large ones.

6. ANNUAL PARLIAMENTS, thus presenting the most effectual check to bribery and intimidation, since though a constituency might be bought once in seven years (even with the ballot), no purse could buy a constituency (under a system of universal suffrage) in each ensuing twelvemonth; and since members, when elected for a year only, would not be able to defy and betray their constituents as now.

What was the significance of their dispersal?
5 Why do some people claim that 'Chartism was laughed into failure'?
6 Explain why the movement had few supporters after 1850.

[11]
1 When did point 1 become law? How far was this aim realised in (i) 1867, (ii) 1884? How did Parliament exceed this demand in 1928?
2 When was point 2 achieved? How did the realisation of this aim help (i) Parnell in Ireland, (ii) the emergence of a working class political party?
3 When was point 4 achieved?
4 Which point has not been achieved?
5 Why did the Charter refer to *seven years*? When and how was this electoral requirement changed?
6 Why did the working classes prefer the Anti-Corn Law League to Chartism?

Topic 6 Palmerston

1 The Quadruple Alliance, 1834

I have been very busy this month, working out my quadruple alliance between England, France, Spain and Portugal, for the expulsion of Carlos and Miguel from the Portugese dominions. It will settle Portugal, and go some way to settle Spain also. But, what is of more importance, it establishes a quadruple alliance among the constitutional states of the west, which will serve as a powerful counterpoise to the Holy Alliance of the east. I should like to see Metternich's face when he reads our treaty.

(Palmerston's letter to his brother, 21 April 1834)

2 Turkish weakness, 1832

The Turkish Empire has reached that critical point at which it must either revive or fall into a state of complete dissolution. To Great Britain, the fate of this Empire can never be indifferent. It would affect the interests of her trade and East Indian Possessions. More pressing duties may forbid H. M. Government to take an active part in the Contest which now agitates Turkey; but the issue can hardly be left to chance on any sound Principle of English Policy.

The principal difficulties with which the Sultan has to contend against Mehemet Ali, arise out of the distant position of Egypt, the ease with which Syria can be defended against an army invading from the North and the disadvantages of having a Fleet which, though superior in numerical Force to that of Egypt, is by no means so well manned and manoeuvred.

In one respect, however, the prospect is clear. Let Mehemet Ali succeed in constituting an Independent State and a great and irretrievable step is made towards the dismemberment of the Turkish Empire. That Empire may fall to pieces, and he must be a bold man who would undertake to answer for its being saved by any effort of human policy. But to leave it to itself is to leave it to its enemies.

(Stratford Canning to Palmerston, 19 December 1832)

3 Unkiar Skelessi

By virtue of article I of the treaty of defensive alliance the Sublime Porte and the Imperial Court of Russia promise to give each other the most effective assistance for the safety of their respective states. His Majesty the Emperor of all the Russias will not demand this help. Instead the

[1]
1 Who were *Carlos and Miguel*?
2 Which powers made up *the Holy Alliance of the east*? Why would Metternich be annoyed by the treaty?
3 What were the main differences between the states in this Quadruple Alliance and the states in the Holy Alliance?

[2]
1 What events of (i) 1825–9, (ii) 1832–3, showed that the decline of Turkey had reached a *critical point*?
2 What *pressing duties* in June 1832 prevented the British Government from taking *an active part* in Turkish affairs?
3 Who was Mehemet Ali? Why did he go to war against the Sultan in 1832?
4 How do you explain the early success of Mehemet Ali in 1832–3?
5 Which other peoples might seek their independence if Mehemet Ali succeeded in his war against Turkey? Why would this be welcome to *Britain's enemies*? Which enemy in particular might have gained an advantage from their independence?

[3]
1 Why did Turkey have to ask for help in (i) 1825, and (ii) 1832–3?
2 Why was it surprising that Turkey asked for *Russian* help in 1833?
3 Why was it surprising that

Ottoman Sublime Porte should confine her activities in favour of Russia, to closing the Strait of the Dardanelles; she will not allow any foreign warships to enter it under any pretext whatsoever.

(Secret article of the Treaty of Unkiar Skelessi, 1833)

4 Palmerston and the Straits, 1840

I have been endeavouring for some months past, in conjunction with Austria, Russia and Prussia, to persuade the French Government to come in to some plan of arrangement between the Sultan and Mehemet Ali. The British Government now has to decide whether the four Powers having failed in persuading France to join them, will or will not proceed without the assistance of France.

The immediate result of our declining to go on with the three Powers because France does not join us will be, that Russia will withdraw her offers to unite with the other Powers for a settlement of the affairs of Turkey, and she will again resume her separate position with respect to those affairs; and you will have the Treaty of Unkiar Skelessi renewed under some still more objectionable form.

The ultimate results of such a decision will be the practical division of the Turkish empire into two states; one will be a dependency of France, and the other a satellite of Russia; and in both our political influence will be annulled, and our commercial interests will be sacrificed; and this dismemberment will inevitably give rise to local struggles and conflicts which will involve the Powers of Europe in most serious disputes.

(Palmerston's letter to Melbourne, 5 July 1840)

5 Mehemet Ali

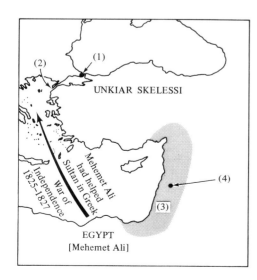

UNKIAR SKELESSI

Mehemet Ali had helped the Sultan in Greek War of Independence 1825–1827

EGYPT
[Mehemet Ali]

Russia agreed to help to maintain the power of the Sultan? How did Russia propose to deal with Turkey in the 'sick man talks'?
4 Why did Russia want the Strait closed to foreign warships?

[4]
1 Who was the French King in 1840? Why might Britain have expected his co-operation in 1840?
2 Why was there a crisis in Turkish affairs in 1840? What did France hope to gain by playing a part in the solution to that crisis? Why might this have led to an Anglo-French war?
3 Why did France refuse to cooperate with Palmerston?
4 Why did Palmerston fear a Russian solution to the Turkish crisis?
5 Give the names of a battle on (i) land, and (ii) sea which helped to bring this crisis to an end.
6 How did Palmerston use his power in 1840–1 to (i) undo the secret clauses of the Treaty of Unkiar Skelessi, (ii) humiliate France, and (iii) restrain Mehemet Ali?

[5]
The questions are based on the map.
1 Why was the area marked 3 a cause of war between Turkey and Mehemet Ali in 1839? What advantages did Mehemet Ali have in that war? Why was Russia entitled to interfere on Turkey's side? What were Palmerston's fears concerning (i) the consequences of Mehemet Ali's success, (ii) Russian interference?
2 Which battle took place near the city marked 4? Why was this battle important for (i) Mehemet Ali, (ii) the future of the Dardanelles, (iii) Anglo-France relations in the 1840s?
3 Why was Britain interested in the control of the area marked 2? How was that control affected by (i) a Treaty signed in 1833, and (ii) a Convention signed in 1841?
4 Which city is on the site marked 1? Why was the British Ambassador in this capital able to exercise great power before the telegraph was invented? How did Canning use this power in 1852–3?

6 Palmerston the patriot

Our guiding rule is to promote and advance the interests of the country to which we have the good fortune to belong. We have no everlasting union with this or that country—no identification of policy with another. We have no natural enemies—no perpetual friends. When we find a Power pursuing a policy which we wish also to promote, that Power becomes our ally; and when we find a country whose interests are at variance with our own, we are involved for a time with the Government of that country. We find no fault with other nations for pursuing their interests; and they ought not to find fault with us if, in pursuing our interests, our course may be different from theirs.

(Palmerston in the House of Commons, 16 May 1848)

[6]
1 With which countries did Britain have an alliance in 1848?
2 Which country did Canning think was Britain's natural enemy? How and why had Palmerston co-operated with that country between 1839 and 1841?
3 How did Palmerston's relations with Louis Philippe bear out the claims made in this passage?
4 How did Palmerston's reactions to the Treaty of Unkiar Skelessi show that he did find fault with other nations for pursuing their interests?

7 Palmerston the bully

The Time is fast coming when we shall be obliged to strike another Blow in China. These half-civilised Governments such as those of China, Portugal, Spanish America, all require a dressing every eight or ten years to keep them in order. Their minds are too shallow to receive an Impression that will last longer than some such Period and warning is of little use. They care little for words and they must not only see the Stick but actually feel it on their Shoulders before they yield to that only argument which to them brings conviction.

(Palmerston autograph note, 29 September 1850, to Sir George Bingham, quoted in W. C. Costin, *Great Britain and China, 1833–60*)

[7]
1 When and why had Britain previously struck a *Blow in China*?
2 What was the outcome of that first Chinese War?
3 When and why did Britain strike *another Blow in China*?
4 What was the outcome of the second Chinese War?
5 What office did Palmerston hold during that second Chinese War?
6 Palmerston's policy in China has been variously described as that of (i) a patriot, and (ii) a bully. With which opinion do you agree? Why?

8 The Queen dismisses Palmerston, 1851

Antagonism had long existed between Palmerston and the Prince Consort. The Prince could not approve of the restless, interfering, and demonstrative line of policy which the Minister since 1848 had adopted and which offended the Continental Governments. The Prince stood up for the right of supervision and control belonging to the Crown in foreign politics. Since the Dom Pacifico affair in 1850, and his expressions of sympathy for Kossuth and the defeated chiefs on the Continent, Palmerston had become burdensome to his own colleagues.

As early as August, 1850, the Queen had sent a memorandum to the Prime Minister, Lord John Russell, in which she expressed distinct demands with regard to Lord Palmerston's mode of conducting business. The memorandum says, 'The Queen requires, first, that Lord

[8]
1 Who was *the Prince Consort*? Why and how had he earned the nickname of 'the Queen's Permanent Minister'?
2 Who was Kossuth? How, if at all, had Palmerston helped him in 1848–9? How do you explain Palmerston's policy in this regard?
3 What two constitutional rights did the Queen claim?
4 Who was *the President*? What was his *coup d'état*?

Palmerston will distinctly state what he proposes in a given case, in order that the Queen may know as distinctly to what she is giving her Royal sanction. Secondly, having once given her sanction to a measure, that it be not arbitrarily altered or modified by the Minister. Such an act she must consider as . . . justly to be visited by the exercise of her constitutional right of dismissing that Minister. The Queen thinks it best that Lord John Russell should show this letter to Lord Palmerston.'

Immediately after the coup d'état the Queen and the Prince discussed the line of policy to be observed by England with regard to this event. It was settled that it must be a policy of abstinence and of neutrality. The Queen wrote in this sense to Lord John Russell, who, in a letter, declared his entire agreement.

But at the same time the French Ambassador in London had informed his Government of a conversation with Lord Palmerston, in which the latter had expressed his 'entire approval' of the coup d'état and his 'conviction' that the President could have acted in no other way. This led to the Premier, Lord John Russell, demanding a written explanation from Lord Palmerston, who, at the same time, received a message in writing, from the Queen, expressing the same request. Lord Palmerston allowed four days to go by without sending his answer, which naturally could not be satisfactory.

(Baron E. von Stockmar, *Memoirs of Baron Stockmar*, edited F. Max Muller, 1872)

5 How and when did Palmerston get his 'tit for tat' with 'little Johnny Russell'?

9 The French Porcupine

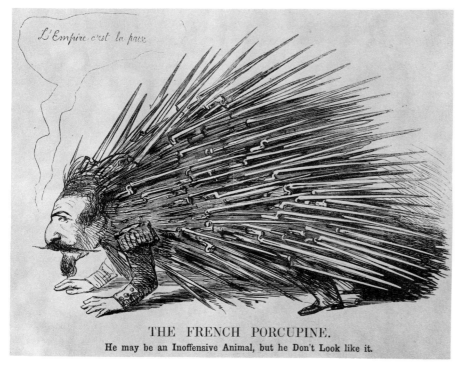

THE FRENCH PORCUPINE.
He may be an Inoffensive Animal, but he Don't Look like it.

L'Empire c'est la paix

[9]
1 Which *Empire* does this cartoon refer to?
2 What had been Palmerston's attitude towards the ruler of that Empire in (i) 1848–51, and (ii) 1853–6?
3 Why was he opposed to that Empire's policy in Italy in 1859?
4 Why did Palmerston order the building of defensive forts around British naval dockyards in 1860? Why were these described as 'Palmerston's follies'?
5 Why was he opposed to the Mexican policy of this Empire?
6 How did this Emperor offend British opinion in his negotiations with Bismark before 1870?

10 A Tory view of the Dom Pacifico affair

It seems that the Athenian mob take great delight on Easter Sunday in burning a representation of Judas Iscariot; but on Easter Sunday, 1847 the Government took measures to prevent the assembling of the people. An opinion arose, however, that M. Pacifico had obtained the discontinuance of this annual celebration, and a mob assembled, and made an attack upon M. Pacifico's house and destroyed what furniture there was in it, and, indeed, everything else. I think that circumstance gives to M. Pacifico a reasonable claim to compensation for those injuries which he sustained in property. But when we come to look at M. Pacifico's bill of costs, it is really one which passes credibility.

Why, the house of this M. Pacifico, who was trading on a borrowed capital of £30, is represented to have been furnished as luxuriously as it might have been if he had been another Aladdin with full command of the Genii of the ring and of the lamp.

(Lord Stanley in the House of Lords, 17 June 1850)

11 Palmerston, the navy and Dom Pacifico

I have desired the Admiralty to instruct Sir William Parker to take Athens on his way back from the Dardanelles, and to support you in bringing at last to a satisfactory ending the settlement of our various claims upon the Greek Government. You will, of course, in conjunction with him, persevere in the negotiations as long as is consistent with our dignity and honour, and I measure that time by days. If, however, the Greek Government does not strike, Parker must do so. In that case you should embark on board his fleet before he begins to take any hostile steps.

(Palmerston's letter to Wyse, the Minister in Athens, December 1849)

12 Palmerston defends himself

The country is told that British subjects in foreign lands are entitled to nothing but the protection of the laws of the land in which they happen to reside, that they must not look to their own country for protection, but must trust to that indifferent justice which they may happen to receive at the hands of the Government of the country in which they may be. Now, I deny that proposition . . . M. Pacifico having been treated either with answer wholly unsatisfactory, or with a positive refusal . . . it came at last to this, either that his demand was to be abandoned altogether, or that we were to proceed to use our own means of enforcing the claim. As the Roman, in days of old, held himself free from indignity, when he could say 'Civis Romanus sum'; so also a British subject, in whatever land he may be, shall feel confident that the watchful eye and the strong arm of England, will protect him against injustice and wrong.

(Palmerston in the House of Commons, 25 June 1850)

[10, 11, 12]
1 Who was *Dom Pacifico*? Why was he entitled to call himself *a British subject*?
2 What was the origin of his claim against the Greek Government? Why did Stanley think it an unreasonable claim?
3 Why was the Greek Government unwilling or unable to agree to that claim?
4 What actions did Palmerston take between December 1849 and March 1850 to further Dom Pacifico's claim?
5 How did Palmerston justify his actions? Do you agree with his argument? Why? With whom was the policy very popular?

13 Palmerston becomes Prime Minister

When Parliament now assembled on January 23 [1855] the House of Commons showed that they reflected faithfully the feverish excitement of the country. Meanwhile, Lord Aberdeen's position was no enviable one. Mr. Roebuck moved for the appointment of a Select Committee to inquire into the conduct of the war, in order to ascertain the causes which had reduced the army in the Crimea to such a miserable plight. That debate ended on the night of January 29 by the motion being carried. There was a majority of 157 against the Ministers.

As the Tories had voted for Roebuck's motion . . . the Queen immediately sent for their leader, Lord Derby. The Earl declined to undertake the responsibility of forming an effective Cabinet at such a critical moment, unless Lord Palmerston would consent to serve with him. The Queen now sent for Lord John Russell. He reaped what he had sown, and was forced in a few days to confess his inability to undertake the Government. Finally the Queen turned to Lord Palmerston. This was a hard resolve to make, but it was a necessity. Palmerston not only had the ear of the House and the favour of the people, but, what was now almost more important than either, the full confidence of Napoleon. There was no disguising the fact that events had to some extent justified Lord Palmerston, and that his over-hasty recognition of the *coup d'état* had rendered possible that alliance which was more necessary now than ever.

(Count Vitzthun, *St Petersburg and London in the Years 1852–64*, 1887)

[13]
1 What were the causes of the *miserable plight* of the British army in the Crimea?
2 How did the British public learn about this plight? What modern invention helped make this possible?
3 What (i) successes, and (ii) failures had the British experienced in the Crimea by 1855?
4 What office had Lord John Russell held in the Aberdeen Government?
5 Why was the Queen reluctant to send for Palmerston?
6 Why was it important that Palmerston had *the full confidence of Napoleon*? What was the significance of the reference to the *coup d'état*?

14 Now for it!

NOW FOR IT!
A Set-to between "Pam, the Downing Street Pet," and "The Russian Spider."

[14]
1 Which crowned monarch was supporting the Russian Spider?
2 Why were the British people anxious for a new policy in 1855? Why did they expect to get it?
3 Outline the course of events in the Crimea during 1855 and 1856. How far, if at all, did these events meet the expectations of the British people?

4 By which treaty was this war brought to an end? How far did the treaty (i) weaken Russian power, (ii) affect the future of Italy?
5 When did Russia undo the damage done to her by this treaty?
6 What was the effect of the Crimean War on (i) army reform, (ii) taxation, (iii) reform of the Civil Service?

Topic 7 Trade Unionism

1 Joining a union, 1830

The eyes of the strangers are again bandaged, and they are then made to walk several times round the room, while the members stamp on the floor with their feet. They are then led to the table, upon which the Bible is placed; the right hand of each is placed upon the sacred volume; the bandages are then removed from their eyes, and they take the following oath:

'I, A. N., woolcomber, being in the awful presence of Almighty God, do voluntarily declare that I will persevere in endeavouring to support a brotherhood known by the name of the Friendly Society of Operative Stuff Manufacturers, and other Industrious Operatives, and I solemnly declare and promise that I will never act in opposition to the brotherhood in any of their attempts to support wages, but will, to the utmost of my power, assist them in all lawful and just occasions to obtain a fair remuneration for our labour. And I call upon God to witness this my most solemn declaration, that neither hopes, fears, rewards, punishments, nor even death itself shall ever induce me directly or indirectly to give any information respecting any thing contained in this Lodge, or any similar Lodge connected with the Society; and I will neither write or cause to be written, upon paper, wood, sand, stone, or anything else, whereby it may be known, unless allowed to do so by the proper authorities of the Society. And I will never give my consent to have any money belonging to the Society divided or appropriated to any other purpose than the use of the Society and support of the trade, so help me God, and keep me steadfast in this my most solemn obligation; and if ever I reveal either part or parts of this my most solemn obligation, may all the Society I am about to belong to, and all that is just, disgrace me so long as I live; and may what is now before me plunge my soul into the everlasting pit of misery. Amen.'

(E. C. Tufnell, *The Character, Objects and Effects of Trades Unions*, 1834)

[1]

1 Why did the early unions have a ceremony of oath-taking? What does this tell you about workers' fears about forming or joining trade unions?

2 Which part of the oath was specifically forbidden by the Combination Acts?

3 Who was legally empowered to fix wages in 1799? Why had that system of wage-fixing been possible in, say 1700 but was inappropriate in the economic conditions of 1800?

4 Why was the number of unions increasing at this time? Why were they mainly confined to (i) skilled workmen, and (ii) men from one locality only?

2 The Repeal of the Combination Laws, 1824

Mr. Francis Place called in and examined.

Have you had much experience with respect to combination of workmen? Yes. I was for some years a journeyman myself, and got sadly punished by the masters combining not to employ me; this was for having interfered in a combination of the men. I afterwards formed several clubs, for the purpose of compelling the masters to give an advance of wages. I thought then, and still think, that it was proper. Wages were very low in some trades, and the workmen had no other means whatever to procure

36

an increase. These combinations of the men were all of them ultimately successful.

What is the system the journeymen tailors now pursue? The system is all but a military system. The orders come from the Executive, and are always obeyed. The whole body never, in any instance, discuss the propriety of a strike, as that would subject them to prosecution under the Combination Laws.

Do the men generally know who are the regulators? No. It is whispered among them that there is to be a strike; but they never discuss the subject; they strike when bid . . .

Do you think the repeal of the Combination Laws would lower wages? No. I think the wages of journeymen tailors, and other workmen, would be just what they are now, except in some few cases, where the Combination Laws have kept them too low. In general, the men have evaded the law and set it totally aside. If the men could legally combine, disputes would seldom occur, but when they did, they would be settled by compromise between the parties. Workmen dread a strike. The influence of the women in the case of a strike is of much importance; they never consent, except in extreme cases.

(Minutes of Select Committee on Artisans and Machinery, February 1824)

[2]

1 Explain the words *master* and *journeyman*. How might a journeyman become a master? Why was this more difficult in 1800 than it had been in, say, 1300?
2 What was the main purpose of the Clubs and combinations? Explain the word *advance*.
3 How successful had the Combination Laws been in banning combinations?
4 What results did Place expect from the repeal of the Laws? Did events prove him right or wrong? What Act concerning trade unions did the Government pass in 1825?

3 The meeting of the Tolpuddle Martyrs, 1834

John Lock. I live at Half Puddle. I know the prisoner, James Brine. He asked me if I would go to Toll Puddle with him. I agreed to do so. James Hammet was then with him. Edward Legg, Richard Peary, Henry Courtney and Elias Riggs were with us. They joined us as we were going along. One of them asked if there would not be something to pay, and one said there would be one shilling to pay on entering and 1d a week after. We all went into Thomas Stanfield's house into a room upstairs. John Stanfield came to the door of the room. I saw James Lovelace and George Lovelace go along the passage. One of the men asked if we were ready. We said, yes. One of them said, 'Then bind your eyes', and we took out handkerchiefs and bound over our eyes. Then they led us into another room on the same floor. Someone then read a paper, but I don't know what the meaning of it was. After that we were asked to kneel down which we did. Then there was some more reading; I don't know what it was about. It seemed to be out of some part of the Bible. Then we got up and took off the bandages from our eyes. I had then seen James Lovelace and John Stanfield in the room. Some one read again, but I don't know what it was and then we were told to kiss the book, when our eyes were unblinded, and I saw the book, which looked like a little Bible. I then saw all the prisoners there. James Lovelace had on a white dress, it was not a smock-frock. They told us the rules, that we should have to pay one shilling then, and a 1d a week afterwards to support the men when they were standing out from their work. They said we were as brothers; that when we were to stop for wages we should not tell our masters ourselves, but that the masters would have a note or a letter sent to them.

(*The Times*, 20 March 1834)

4 The warning by Dorchester magistrates, 1834

CAUTION.

WHEREAS it has been represented to us from several quarters, that mischievous and designing Persons have been for some time past, endeavouring to induce, and have induced, many Labourers in various Parishes in this County, to attend Meetings, and to enter into Illegal Societies or Unions, to which they bind themselves by unlawful oaths, administered secretly by Persons concealed, who artfully deceive the ignorant and unwary,—WE, the undersigned Justices think it our duty to give this PUBLIC NOTICE and CAUTION, that all Persons may know the danger they incur by entering into such Societies.

ANY PERSON who shall become a Member of such a Society, or take any Oath, or assent to any Test or Declaration not authorized by Law—

Any Person who shall administer, or be present at, or consenting to the administering or taking any Unlawful Oath, or who shall cause such Oath to be administered, although not actually present at the time—

Any Person who shall not reveal or discover any Illegal Oath which may have been administered, or any Illegal Act done or to be done—

Any Person who shall induce, or endeavour to persuade any other Person to become a Member of such Societies,

WILL BECOME

Guilty of Felony,

AND BE LIABLE TO BE

Transported for Seven Years.

ANY PERSON who shall be compelled to take such an Oath, unless he shall declare the same within four days, together with the whole of what he shall know touching the same, will be liable to the same Penalty.

Any Person who shall directly or indirectly maintain correspondence or intercourse with such Society, will be deemed Guilty of an Unlawful Combination and Confederacy, and on Conviction before one Justice, on the Oath of one Witness, be liable to a Penalty of TWENTY POUNDS, or to be committed to the Common Gaol or House of Correction, for THREE CALENDAR MONTHS; or if proceeded against by Indictment, may be CONVICTED OF FELONY, and be TRANSPORTED FOR SEVEN YEARS.

Any Person who shall knowingly permit any Meeting of any such Society to be held in any House, Building, or other Place, shall for the first offence be liable to the Penalty of FIVE POUNDS; and for every other offence committed after Conviction, be deemed Guilty of such Unlawful Combination and Confederacy, and on Conviction before one Justice, on the Oath of one Witness, be liable to a Penalty of TWENTY POUNDS, or to Commitment to the Common Gaol or House of Correction, FOR THREE CALENDAR MONTHS; or if proceeded against by Indictment may be

CONVICTED OF FELONY,

And Transported for SEVEN YEARS.

COUNTY OF DORSET, Dorchester Division

February 22d, 1834.

C. B. WOLLASTON,
JAMES FRAMPTON,
WILLIAM ENGLAND,
THOS. DADE,
JNO. MORTON COLSON.

HENRY FRAMPTON,
RICHD. TUCKER STEWARD,
WILLIAM R. CHURCHILL,
AUGUSTUS FOSTER.

G. CLARK, PRINTER, CORNHILL, DORCHESTER.

[3, 4]

1 What was the official position of the people who signed this notice? What part had such people played in (i) wage-fixing, and (ii) the Peterloo massacre of 1819?

2 Which factory owner led the Grand National Consolidated Union in 1834? How did this union differ from previous unions as regards (i) the trade or craft of members, and (ii) the localities from which members were drawn?

3 Which of the aims of the union were specifically forbidden by an Act passed in 1825?

4 For which of their activities were the members of the union liable to be prosecuted? When and why had such activity been made illegal?

5 Who was Home Secretary at this time? What attitude did he take towards the sentences passed on the Tolpuddle Martyrs?

6 What was meant by *Transported*? Why would such a punishment often mean a life sentence?

7 What was the ultimate fate of the Tolpuddle Martyrs? How far does their case help to explain the failure of the union?

5 Employers versus trade unions, 1832

'We, the undersigned, agree with Messrs . . . that we will work for them on the following terms:

'We declare that we do not belong to the 'Union' or any other society which has for its object any interference with the rules laid down for the government of mills. We agree with our masters that we will not become members of any such society while in our present employ. We will not subscribe or contribute to any such society, or to any striking hands whatsoever. And if we are discovered to act contrary to the above agreement, each of us so offending will forfeit a sum equal to a fortnight's wages.'

(Evidence to a Parliamentary Committee, 1831–2)

[5]

1 Who made *the rules laid down for the government of mills*? Why did the former domestic workers resent such rules? Why were they needed if the mills and factories were to run economically?

2 How might the 'Union' have tried to interfere with those rules?

3 Why were many workmen willing to sign such a document? What does this tell you of

6 A miner remembers a strike, 1844

There was no eagerness for a strike, for there were no defensive resources. The tommy shops, the only shops where miners' families had been able to obtain food, would close. There were no co-operative societies with little saved-up balances to the name of each member. The union had no reserve fund. So methods of conciliation were resorted to. On March 20, 1844, the men sent a letter to the owners asking them to receive a deputation from the Miners' Association. There was no reply of any sort.

(Aaron Watson, *The Life of Thomas Burt*, 1908)

7 During the strike

The mine owners got together enough men of one sort or another, to set the mines going again. As soon as the strangers arrived they needed houses, and as the men on strike still occupied the cottages, the work of ejecting them now commenced. Bands of policemen, with low, mean ragged fellows were ordered into the miners' houses and, 'Will you go to work?' was asked of the pitman. The answer being 'No!' orders were given to remove everything. The yelling and shouting and the pitiful cries of the children had no effect. The furniture was removed into the lanes.

Sentries patrolled the pits for the protection of the engines and premises, and the men who were at work; each night the country was scoured by squadrons of cavalry.

8 After the strike

Numbers were refused work, generally those who had taken a leading part in the strike. Mr. Haswell was one. He and his father travelled round a great number of collieries in the two counties, and in many places, though men were wanted, they would not give them employment. It was evident the name was on the 'black books'.

The men who had been on strike and those who had been at work during the strike as 'blacklegs' never met on friendly terms and the former gave indications that they would have a day of reckoning. On 15th August a great riot occurred. Hundreds of men had drawn together, including English, Welsh and Irish, and a pitched battle began. They tore off the garden railings, got pick shafts and anything that would deal a blow. Soon every lane was thronged with reinforcements from other collieries. The Welshmen finally fled, making their escape over the railway and into their houses. Rumours were raised that soldiers were coming, and but for this the English would have followed and destroyed them and their houses. As it was, great numbers were wounded and severely injured on both sides.

(J. Fynes, *Miners of Northumberland and Durham*, 1875)

the comparative power of masters and workmen?

4 Workmen in some factories refused to sign such documents. How did their masters treat employees in that case? Why did this often lead to outbreaks of violence?

[6, 7, 8]

1 What were *tommy shops*? Why were they more common in mining villages than in larger industrial towns?

2 How might a *co-operative* have helped the striking miners?

3 Who were *the strangers*? Why were they willing to work in strike-bound pits?

4 Why did the owners have the legal right to evict their striking workmen? Why did they wish to do so?

5 Why did the miners lose their strike in 1844?

9 Applegarth on the benefits paid by the Amalgamated Society of Carpenters and Joiners

What are the objects of your associations?—The object of this society is to raise funds for the mutual support of its members in case of sickness, accident, superannuation, for the burial of members and their wives, emigration, loss of tools by fire, water or theft, and for assistance to members out of work. These are the objects of the society as stated in the preamble of the rules.

Does 1s. a week entitle a man to all the benefits you have specified?—A shilling per week and 3d per quarter to a benevolent and contingent fund. The benefits are as follows: Unemployment benefit for 12 weeks, 10s. per week; and for another 12 weeks, 6s. per week; sick benefit for 26 weeks, 12s. per week, and then 6s. per week so long as his illness continues; funeral benefit 12l., or 31.10s. when a six months member dies; accident benefit, 100l.; superannuation benefit for life, if a member 25 years, 8s. per week; if a member 18 years, 7s. per week; if a member for 12 years, 5s. per week. The emigration benefit is 6l., and there are benevolent grants, according to circumstances, in cases of distress.

(Evidence to Royal Commission on Trade Unions, 18 March 1867)

10 William Allen, secretary of the Amalgamated Society of Engineers, on strikes

What do you consider is the reason of the fact, that you have had no strike of any consequence since 1852?—The Executive Council, and the members, generally speaking, are averse to strikes. They think that matters ought to be settled in a different way than coming to strikes or lock-outs.

What measures have men to take before they can strike in your society?—They have to represent their grievances to the committee of their branch. In a town where there is more than one branch there is what is called a district committee, composed of members from the different branches, and instead of the branch committee dealing with the question the district committee deals with it.

Therefore, unless approved of in the first place by the branches of their own town, and in the second place by the central executive council, no members of your trade can strike?—No.

(Evidence to Royal Commission, 1867)

[9,10]

1 What is the significance of the word *Amalgamated* in the title of these unions?
2 What is the significance of the words *of Carpenters and Joiners* and *of Engineers*, in the titles of these unions? Why did they have comparatively few members in the 1850s and 1860s?
3 Why were such unions called Model Unions? How did they differ from the larger union which collapsed after the Tollpuddle affair?
4 In what ways did these unions try to perform the functions of a welfare state for their members? Why could they afford to do so?
5 Why were the leaders of Model Unions unwilling to spend their funds on strikes? How did they (i) deal with employers, and (ii) control their more militant members?
6 Applegarth, Allen and other national secretaries were nick-named 'the Junta'. Why? What were their political aims? How far were they successful?

[11]

1 What is a *Trades Council*? Name two of the leaders of the London Trades Council in 1868.
2 What is the significance of item 11 of the proposed agenda? Why did many trade unionists think that there might be 'a measure detrimental to the interests of such Societies'?
3 How far, if at all, were these fears justified by the laws which followed the Report of the Royal Commission?
4 Why did the *Congress* meet in Manchester, not London?

PROPOSED CONGRESS OF TRADES COUNCILS

AND OTHER

Federations of Trades Societies.

———————◦◦◦◦◦———————

MANCHESTER, FEBRUARY 21st, 1868.

FELLOW-UNIONISTS,

The Manchester and Salford Trades Council having recently taken into their serious consideration the present aspect of Trades Unions, and the profound ignorance which prevails in the public mind with reference to their operations and principles, together with the probability of an attempt being made by the Legislature, during the present session of Parliament, to introduce a measure detrimental to the interests of such Societies, beg most respectfully to suggest the propriety of holding in Manchester, as the main centre of industry in the provinces, a Congress of the Representatives of Trades Councils and other similar Federations of Trades Societies. By confining the Congress to such bodies it is conceived that a deal of expense will be saved, as Trades will thus be represented collectively; whilst there will be a better opportunity afforded of selecting the most intelligent and efficient exponents of our principles.

It is proposed that the Congress shall assume the character of the annual meetings of the British Association for the Advancement of Science and the Social Science Association, in the transactions of which Societies the artizan class are almost entirely excluded; and that papers, previously carefully prepared, shall be laid before the Congress on the various subjects which at the present time affect Trades Societies, each paper to be followed by discussion upon the points advanced, with a view of the merits and demerits of each question being thoroughly ventilated through the medium of the public press. It is further suggested that the subjects treated upon shall include the following :—

1.—Trades Unions an absolute necessity.
2.—Trades Unions and Political Economy.
3.—The Effect of Trades Unions on Foreign Competition.
4.—Regulation of the Hours of Labour.
5.—Limitation of Apprentices.
6.—Technical Education.
7.—Arbitration and Courts of Conciliation.
8.—Co-operation.
9.—The present Inequality of the Law in regard to Conspiracy, Intimidation, Picketing, Coercion, &c.
10.—Factory Acts Extension Bill, 1867: the necessity of Compulsory Inspection, and its application to all places where Women and Children are employed.
11.—The present Royal Commission on Trades Unions: how far worthy of the confidence of the Trades Union interest.
12.—The necessity of an Annual Congress of Trade Representatives from the various centres of industry.

All Trades Councils and other Federations of Trades are respectfully solicited to intimate their adhesion to this project on or before the 6th of April next, together with a notification of the subject of the paper that each body will undertake to prepare; after which date all information as to place of meeting, &c., will be supplied.

It is also proposed that the Congress be held on the 4th of May next, and that all liabilities in connection therewith shall not extend beyond its sittings.

Communications to be addressed to MR. W. H. WOOD, Typographical Institute, 29, Water Street, Manchester.

By order of the Manchester and Salford Trades Council,

S. C. NICHOLSON, PRESIDENT.
W. H. WOOD, SECRETARY.

12 The dockers' strike, 1889

The strike will remain a most significant event in the relations between capital and labour. The despised dock labourers, possessed of no special skill, have been able to combine. But this was by no means the most remarkable phenomenon of the strike. If the dock labourers and their employers had been left alone to fight it out the dock labourers could not have held out for a week. The hard case of the men elicited the sympathy of all the various categories of riverside labourers without exception. These among them made up a compact industrial army, without whom the shipping trade of London could not proceed. More than that, the case of the dock labourers drew sympathy and material support from all quarters. Thus the men were placed beyond the reach of starvation. The hints afforded by the great strike will probably not be neglected in the future. We may look for a large development of future conflicts between capital and labour.

(*The Times*, 16 September 1889)

13 New Unionism, 1889–1900

The formation of our union was the beginning of what has been termed the 'New Unionism'. It was the culmination of long years of Socialist propaganda amongst the underpaid workers. We offered them a definite road out of their misery, a trade union that would improve their wages and conditions. They came in thousands; within six months we had made over 20,000 members in different parts of the country. We showed the way to the dockers and other unskilled workers; our example and our success gave them hope. Within a short time the 'New Unionism' was in full flower. It changed the whole face of the British Trade Union Movement, a movement that had mainly consisted of liberal-minded craftsmen and skilled unionists. The growth and development of our union and the dockers and others that followed us brought to the Trade Union Congress a new force. It established on a firm footing the political Labour Movement.

(Will Thorne, *My Life's Battles*, 1924)

14 The Taff Vale decision, 1901

The judgement makes no change in the lawfulness of Trade Unionism. No act is made wrongful which was not wrongful before. If a Trade Union causes damage, it seems fair that it should be liable for what it has done. The grievance of the Trade Union lies in the uncertainty of the English law, and its liability to be used as a means of oppression. This is increased by the dislike of Trade Unionism which nearly all judges and juries share with the rest of the upper and middle classes.

The middle classes are more hostile to Trade Unionism than a generation ago. In 1867–75, when Trade Unionism was struggling for

[12]

1 Why had the dock labourers been despised by other workmen? What was the significance of their combination?
2 Name two of the men, other than Burns, largely responsible for bringing out *all the various categories of riverside labourers*.
3 How did Burns help the dockers to win the sympathy of many Londoners?
4 What *material support* was provided by Australian dockers? Why was such help of great importance to the families of the striking men?
5 How was the strike settled? How far were the men successful?

[13]

1 How did *New Unionism* differ from the *Old* as regards (i) the type of worker–member, (ii) numbers, (iii) funds, and (iv) militancy?
2 Name two societies which were preaching *Socialist propaganda*. Which was thought to be the most socialist of the existing societies?
3 Why did the members of the craft unions not feel the need for a *political Labour Movement*? Which of the existing political parties did they tend to support?
4 Why did the unskilled need such a political movement?

[14]

1 What was the origin of the Taff Vale dispute? Why did it involve the Amalgamated Society of Railway Servants?
2 How had trade unions benefited from legislation passed between 1867 and 1875? Why had that legislation depended on the support of the middle classes?

legal recognition, it seemed only fair that the workmen should be put in a position to make a good fight of it against the employers. Accordingly, combinations, strikes and peaceful picketing were legalised. It all belonged to the conception of a labour dispute as a fight between the parties, in which the State could do no more than keep the ring. Gradually this has given way to the view that the stoppage of work by an industrial dispute is a public nuisance, which ought to be prevented by the Government. Public opinion has become uneasy about the capacity of English manufacturers to hold their own against foreign competition, and therefore resents any attempt to restrict output or obstruct machinery, of which the Trade Unions may be accused.

(S. and B. Webb, *Industrial Democracy*, 1902)

15 Unions and political funds, 1910

House of Commons, 22 November 1910

Mr. G. N. Barnes: I desire to ask the Prime Minister a question of which I have given him private notice, namely, whether the Government have yet had the opportunity of discussing the further attitude to be adopted on the Osborne Judgement?

The Prime Minister: I have already indicated the intention of the Government in regard to payment of Members and official election expenses. We shall further propose legislation empowering trade unions to include in their objects and organisation the provision of a fund for Parliamentary and municipal action and representation and kindred objects, and to combine for such purposes, provided that the opinion of the union is effectively ascertained, and that there shall be no compulsion upon any member to contribute to the fund.

Mr. Arthur Henderson: Arising out of the latter part of the Prime Minister's answer, are we to understand that no member being compelled to subscribe there is going to be some provisions for a member to contract out?

The Prime Minister: There is no necessity for contracting out.

Mr. Keir Hardie: Can the right hon. gentleman say what is meant by no compulsion? Is a member to be free to reclaim the amount of his contribution which might be applied for political purposes?

The Prime Minister: No, Sir. He is not to be penalised or in any way injuriously affected if he refuses to pay.

Mr. Keir Hardie: May I ask, in the case of those unions—which are in a large majority—where there is no special levy for political purposes, and where the Parliamentary fund is taken out of the general funds of the union, what is to be the procedure?

The Prime Minister: . . . it shall become one of the lawful objects of trade unions to provide a fund—by which I mean a separate fund.

Mr. Keir Hardie: Does that mean specifically that the union shall not be free to use its ordinary funds for political purposes, and must a political fund be raised by means of a special levy?

The Prime Minister: Yes, I think that follows.

(Hansard, 1910, vol. 20)

3 Why were trade unions more unpopular in 1901 than they had been in 1875? Why were middle classes more hostile in 1901 than they had been in 1875?

4 What did the Taff Vale judgement say? How might this have been used *as a means of oppression*?

5 How did the Taff Vale judgement affect the growth of the Labour Party? Why?

6 To whom did the Society have to pay the £23,000? What other payments did the Society have to make at the same time?

[15]

1 Who was Osborne? What was the *Osborne Judgement*? How did it affect the development of the Labour Party?

2 Who was the Prime Minister in 1909?

3 What did the Government do about the *payment of Members*? When? Why was this more important to the Labour Party than to the other two Parties?

4 What new legal power was given to trade unions after the Osborne Judgement? On what two conditions could unions exercise that power?

5 What was meant by *contracting out*? Why did relatively few members contract out?

6 When were these proposals passed into law?

Topic 8 Gladstone

1 Gladstone and retrenchment

If you want to benefit the labouring classes and to do the maximum amount of good you should extend the area of trade by steadily removing restrictions. I rank the introduction of cheap postage for letters and the abolition of all taxes on printed matter in the catalogue of free trade legislation. These great measures may well take their place beside the abolition of prohibitions and protective duties as forming together the great code of industrial emancipation.

(Gladstone in an article written in 1880)

2 The political catechism

NEW POLITICAL CATECHISM

THIRD EDITION.

WITH EMENDATIONS AND CORRECTIONS BY "TRUTH."

Granted that the Expenditure of the Liberals in 1861 was £73,000,000, what was it in 1865 -	£66,000,000
What was the Income Tax when the Liberals took Office in 1861? - - - - -	10d. in the £
What was it in 1865 when they left Office? - - - - - -	4d. in the £
What is it now under Tory management? - - - - -	6d. in the £
Who are the men that proposed to charter a Roman Catholic University in Ireland by a further grant of Money? -	THE TORIES
Who are they that seek to perpetuate an injustice like the Irish Church - -	THE TORIES
Who opposed the admission of Dissenters to the Universities? - -	THE TORIES
Who abolished the Compound Rating Clause, thus compelling personal payment of Rates?	THE TORIES
Who gave the Nation a uniform Penny Postage? - - - - -	THE LIBERALS
Who reduced the National Debt £12,000,000? - - - -	THE LIBERALS
Who reduced the Duty on Tea from 2s. 2d. to 6d. per lb.? - -	THE LIBERALS
Who reduced the Duties on Sugar, Wine, and Hops? - -	THE LIBERALS
Who reduced the Duty on Coffee from 6d. to 3d. per lb.? - -	THE LIBERALS
Who reduced the Duty on Fire Insurance from 3s. to 1s. 6d. per cent., and intend to abolish it altogether?	THE LIBERALS
Who repealed the Duties on Soap, Bricks, Timber and Paper? - -	THE LIBERALS
Who abolished compulsory Church Rates? (Gladstone) - - -	THE LIBERALS
Who amended and improved the so far good, but still imperfect, measure of Reform, and carried it too?	THE LIBERALS
From these facts and many others, which could be quoted, it must be clear to all, that the true friends of the Country are	THE LIBERALS
And to them only can we look for any reduction of Taxation, or removal of Burdens from the People.	

☞ **Electors!** ponder on these things, talk them over amongst yourselves when you meet together, and by your own firesides, and you must come to the conclusion that the Conservatives are not the men you ought to support, but **THE LIBERALS!**

[1]

1 Why would *removing restrictions* help to *extend the area of trade*?

2 Which Civil Servant had been largely responsible for *the introduction of cheap postage*? When? How did the new system differ from the old? How far was the emergence of cheap postage dependent on the development of railways?

3 When had Gladstone removed *all taxes on printed matter*? How did this affect the price of newspapers? What other reasons can you offer to account for the increased sale of newspapers in the last quarter of the nineteenth century?

4 Which social classes benefited from reductions in (i) income tax, (ii) duties? How far does this help to explain the Liberal victory in 1868? Why did many former Liberals support the Tories in the 1874 Election?

[2]

1 How did the *Catechism* explain the rise in the consumption of *tea* and *sugar*? Can you think of other reasons for those rises?

2 Why is *Income Tax* called a direct tax? Which classes in Great Britain in the 1860s paid that tax? Why might they have been expected to support *the Liberals*?

3 Why are taxes on goods (tea, soap etc) called indirect taxes? Which classes paid those taxes? Why might they have been expected to support *the Liberals*?

4 Which Ministers in the 1820s and 1840s had lowered indirect taxes? To which party had they belonged?

5 Explain *Dissenters*. Why were they not allowed to go to *the Universities*? When and by which government was the law on University entrance changed?

3 Joseph Chamberlain and social reform

We bring up a population in dreary, filthy courts and alleys and place them under conditions in which the observance of even ordinary decency is impossible. It is no more the fault of these people that they are vicious and intemperate than it is their fault that they are stunted, and diseased.

We cannot afford any longer to stand with folded arms in the presence of so great an evil. To do so would be a positive danger to the State; for there is a danger in this ever widening contrast between the wealth of a few individuals and the deepening squalor of a large class of the population. Something must be done quickly, if our boasted prosperity is to rest upon its only sure foundation—the happiness, of the whole community.

We must endeavour to get all the houses made fit for people to live in.

(Joseph Chamberlain in *The New Review*, 1895)

[3]

1 Why were the majority of the working class forced to live in *dreary, filthy courts*? Why could a minority of workers afford better housing? What societies did they found to help them to do so?

2 How far were housing and sanitary conditions improved by Acts passed by (i) Gladstone, (ii) Disraeli? Why was such legislation unpopular with many ratepayers?

3 What part had Chamberlain played in improving conditions in Birmingham?

4 What *danger* did Chamberlain foresee for (i) the State, and (ii) the people if more reforms were not undertaken?

4 Chamberlain and increased taxation, 1885

I have been criticised for saying that the rich pay too little and the poor pay too much. In my opinion there is only one way in which this can be remedied, and that is by some scheme of graduated taxation.

I would tax all unoccupied and sporting land at its full value and insist on a restitution to the community of inclosures which have been illegally made. The sanctity of property is no doubt an important principle, but the public good is a greater and a higher object than any private interest.

I do not say that every one of these points is necessarily an article in the Liberal programme, but the Liberal party has been a popular party . . . reinforced from time to time by successive Reform Bills; and now after the greatest of them all it would be false to its trust and unworthy of its mission if it did not strive to bring the institutions of the country into harmony with the wants and aspirations of the people.

(Joseph Chamberlain quoted in *The Times*, 6 August 1885)

[4, 5]

1 Which taxes were paid, in the main, by the poor? Which taxes were paid, almost entirely, by the rich? Which of these did Chamberlain want to tax more heavily? Why did this drive many former Liberals into the Conservative camp?

2 What is meant by *graduated taxation*? When and how did Lloyd George introduce this system into the British taxation system?

3 How would Chamberlain have spent more money to help solve the problems of (i) squalor, (ii) ignorance, and (iii) the poverty of old people?

4 Which *Reform Bills* did Chamberlain have in mind? Which did he think was *the greatest of them all*?

5 Why did Gladstone disagree with Chamberlain's proposals? Why were millions of people unable to follow Gladstone's advice to help themselves?

5 Gladstone opposes Chamberlain, 1885

There is a disposition to think that the Government ought to do this and that, and that the Government ought to do everything. If the Government takes into its hand that which the man ought to do for himself, it will inflict upon him greater mischiefs than all the benefits he will have received. The spirit of self-reliance should be preserved in the minds of the masses of the people, in the minds of every member of that class.

(Gladstone speaking in Edinburgh, September, 1885)

6 Chamberlain attacks Gladstone, 1885

It is therefore perfectly futile and ridiculous for any political Rip Van Winkle to come down from the mountain on which he has been slumbering and to tell us that these things are to be excluded from the Liberal programme. We have to account for and to grapple with the mass of misery and destitution in our midst. I shall be told tomorrow that this is Socialism. Of course, it is Socialism. The greater part of municipal work is Socialism, and every kindly act of legislation by which the community has sought to discharge its responsibilities and its obligations to the poor is Socialism, but it is none the worse for that. Our object is the elevation of the poor, of the masses of the people.

(Joseph Chamberlain quoted in *The Times*, 9 September 1885)

[6]
1 What political event was the occasion for the speeches in items 5 and 6? To which group was Chamberlain appealing for support?
2 What position had Chamberlain occupied between 1880 and 1885? Why did this enable him to learn a good deal about poverty?
3 What was meant by *municipal work*? In what ways was this *Socialism*? Why has that *work* been described as 'Gas and Water Socialism' and as 'environmental reform'? Who, in particular, had argued for such work between 1834 and 1854?
4 Give three examples of what Chamberlain meant by *these things*. Why were these proposals described as *Socialism*? Why have they sometimes been described as 'personal socialism'?

7 In praise of Gladstone's career

To me, Gladstone's life is specially interesting as that of a man who was a fearless and powerful upholder of humanity and righteousness in an age in which faith in both was growing weak, and Jingoism, with its lust for war and rapine, was taking possession of the world. The man who, breaking through the restraints of diplomatic prudery, pleaded before Europe with prevailing eloquence the cause of oppressive Italy, who dared, after Majuba Hill, in face of public excitement, to keep the path of justice and honour in dealing with the Transvaal; whose denunciation of the Bulgarian atrocities made the Turkish Assassin tremble on his throne in iniquity . . . has a more peculiar hold on my veneration and gratitude than the statesman, whose achievements and merits have never seemed to me quite so great, as in Mr. Morley's admirably executed picture, they appear. Not that I would undervalue Gladstone's statesmanship or its fruits. Wonderful improvements in finance, great administrative reforms, the opening of the Civil Service, the Postal Savings Bank, the liberation of the newspaper press from the paper duty, the abolition of purchase in the Army, the reform of the Universities followed by that of the endowed schools, the disestablishment of the Irish Church, and the Commercial Treaty with France, make up a mighty harvest of good work.

(Goldwin Smith, *My Memory of Gladstone*, 1904)

[7]
1 What was meant by *Jingoism*? Why was this a popular policy in the nineteenth century?
2 How did Gladstone *keep the path of justice and honour in dealing with the Transvaal*? Explain the reference to *Majuba Hill*.
3 When did Gladstone denounce *the Bulgarian atrocities*? Explain the reference to the Turkish assassin.
4 How had Gladstone opened *the Civil Service*? Which social class had approved of that reform? Why?
5 Which Minister was responsible for *the abolition of purchase in the Army*? Why did he introduce this reform?

8 The Education Act, 1870

There shall be provided for every school district a sufficient amount of accommodation in public elementary schools for all the children resident in such district for whose elementary education efficient and suitable provision is not otherwise made.

Where the Education Department are satisfied that there is an insufficient amount of public school accommodation for any school district, a school board shall be formed for such district and shall supply such deficiency.

Every public elementary school shall be conducted in accordance with the following regulations, namely,

(i) no child shall be required to attend or to abstain from attending any Sunday school, or any place of religious worship.
(ii) the time or times during which any instruction in religious subjects is given at any meeting of the school shall be either at the beginning of or at the end of such meeting . . . and any scholar may be withdrawn by his parent.
(iii) the school shall be open at all times to the inspection of any of Her Majesty's inspectors.

Every child attending a school provided by any school board shall pay such weekly fee as may be prescribed by the school board, but the school board may remit the whole or any part of such fee in the case of any child when they are of the opinion that the parent of such child is unable from poverty to pay the same.

Every school board . . . may make byelaws

(i) requiring the parents of children of such age, not less than five years nor more than thirteen years, as may be fixed by the byelaws, to cause such children (unless there is some reasonable excuse) to attend school;
(ii) determining the time during which children are so to attend school.

[8]
1 Which two organisations provided most of the schools giving *elementary education* before 1870? Explain *elementary*. Explain *school district*.
2 When could school boards be set up? How were these chosen? How would they get the money they needed to set up board schools?
3 Over which of these clauses did the Anglicans quarrel with the Nonconformists? Why?
4 Why did *the inspection* by one of *Her Majesty's inspectors* take place at least once a year? How did this inspection affect the salary of teachers?
5 How far, if at all, was education (i) free, and (ii) compulsory as a result of this Act?
6 Which Minister was responsible for this Act? What position did he have in the Gladstone Government in 1881?

9 A Gladstone menu, 1881

A Grand Banquet (or General Mess) at the Boers Head Hotel immediately after the sale of the Effects of Mr. John Bull carefully prepared by Mr. W. E. Gladstone.

Soups

Peace Soup   White Liver Soup

Entrées

Irish Stew with Buckshot Sauce   Toady in the Hole

Savouries

Hashed Turkey with Mulled Porte

W(h)ines and other Beverages

The Banqueting Room will be appropriately decorated for the occasion with White Feathers.

(From a broadsheet issued in London, 1881)

[9]
1 Why was there a reference to the *Boers* in this 1881 menu?
2 What was the meaning of *White Liver*? Do you agree with this opinion of Gladstone? Why?
3 Why was there a reference to *Irish Stew*? What was the significance of the word *Buckshot*?
4 What was the *Porte*? What part had Turkish affairs played in Gladstone's election victory in 1880?

47

10 Wait till the clouds roll by, Billy

"WAIT TILL THE CLOUDS ROLL BY!"

[10]

1 Why was *Egypt* a problem in 1885? How far had Gladstone reversed his predecessor's policy in regard to Egypt?
2 Why might the cartoonist have put *Sudan* as a problem?
3 Which *Colonial Difficulties* had Gladstone faced in (i) Asia, (ii) Africa, between 1880 and 1885? How far were his policies in these continents different from those of his predecessor?
4 Why might the cartoonist have put *Ireland* as a problem in January 1885?
5 Who was the leader of the *Opposition*? Who led the Fourth Party?
6 Why did the Opposition of January 1885 form a minority government later that year? What was the result of the Election called by that minority government? What part did Parnell play in ensuring that result?

11 Land tenancy in Ireland, 1879

A twenty-one years' lease granted to the present tenant's father in 1860 fixed the rent at about £410. The son succeeded while this lease was running, and in 1876 or 1877 became anxious for a new lease. The new lease was not granted, and accordingly the tenant sought to register under the Land Act of 1870, his permanent improvements. These improvements were mainly under the following heads: Blasting, sledging and removing stones; levelling old ditches and making new ones; building sewers; making main and minor drains; sinking wells and repairing roads. There were also building improvements . . . there was an enclosure wall, a new granary, steamhouse and cowsheds, workmen's lodge and piggeries. The tenants' accounts showed an expenditure on these and other items of over £2,000.

But the landlord contested the right to register these improvements. A lawsuit arose, which ended with the decision that the improvements could be registered, but not the amount of money spent on them. The lawsuit cost the tenant £500. This lease expired a few months before the Land Act of 1881 was passed. No renewal had taken place, and the tenant was served with a notice of eviction, under the pressure of which he accepted a sixty years' lease at a rent of £380.

(H. S. Wilkinson, *The Eve of Home Rule—Impression of Ireland in 1886*)

[11]

1 Why did Gladstone pass *the Land Act of 1870*? What did this say?
2 Which other Act did Gladstone pass to try to 'pacify Ireland' in his 'Great Ministry'?
3 How does this extract show that the Land Act did not work as well as Gladstone had hoped? Why did few tenants challenge their landlords in the courts?
4 What were the main terms of *the Land Act of 1881*? How would the tenant have benefited from that Act?
5 Explain *eviction*. Why was this often accompanied by violence?
6 What happened to agricultural prices in the 1870s and 1880s? How does this help to explain the lower rent paid on the renewal of the lease?

12 The live shell

PUNCH, OR THE LONDON CHARIVARI.—January 30, 1886.

THE LIVE SHELL.

(WHICH OF 'EM WILL THROW IT OVERBOARD?)

[12]

1 What was the significance of the date on which this cartoon appeared—for Gladstone and for Salisbury?

2 Why was Parnell politically more important in January 1886 than he had been in November 1885?

3 Why did Gladstone hope that Salisbury would deal with the *Irish Question*?

4 How, later, did Salisbury deal with (i) Irish violence, and (ii) Irish tenant farmers?

5 How had Gladstone tried to deal with the *Irish Question* between (i) 1868 and 1874, and (ii) 1880 and 1885? Why had the *Question* still not been answered?

6 How did the attempts to answer the *Question* in 1886 affect Chamberlain's relations with (i) Gladstone, and (ii) Salisbury?

Topic 9
Disraeli

THE RISING GENERATION—IN PARLIAMENT.

Peel. "WELL, MY LITTLE MAN, WHAT ARE YOU GOING TO DO THIS SESSION, EH?"
D——li (the Juvenile). "WHY—AW—AW—I'VE MADE ARRANGEMENTS—AW—TO SMASH—AW—EVERYBODY."

1 The saviour of the Conservatives

Let the Conservative party never forget the hopeless Slough of Despond in which they were wallowing when kind fortune sent them Mr. DISRAELI for a leader. They had grown weary of a chief who was too liberal for their contracted views of national policy, and avenged themselves upon him by an act of renunciation which left them without leaders. They were irretrievably committed to an unpopular cause.

Gradually, Mr. DISRAELI has weaned his party from their most flagrant errors. He has taught them a lesson which they have been slow indeed to learn. He has taught them to profess a sympathy for the great body of their countrymen, and to recognise the necessity of looking to opinion for support. When he found the Tory party they were armed in impenetrable prejudice; under him they have become competitors with the Liberals in the career of progress.

(*The Times*, 6 June 1860)

2 Disraeli and social reform

I am not here to maintain that there is nothing to be done to increase the well-being of the working classes of this country; but in attempting to legislate upon social matters the great object is to be practical—to have before us some distinct aims and some distinct means by which they can be accomplished.

[1]
1 In which session of Parliament and over what issue had Disraeli 'smashed' Peel's Government?
2 Why had this *left them without leaders*? Name three Peelites who served in Whig–Liberal Governments in the 1850s and 1860s.
3 Who, in name, was the leader of the Conservatives in 1860? When did the Conservatives form a government in the 1850s? What position did Disraeli hold? When did he become the leader and Prime Minister?
4 Which *of their countrymen* and which body of opinion could the Conservatives rely on in 1850? Why?
5 Which *opinion* did Disraeli have to win over? Why?

50

I think public attention as regards these matters ought to be concentrated upon sanitary legislation. Pure air, pure water, the inspection of unhealthy habitations, the adulteration of food, these and many kindred matters may be legitimately dealt with by the legislature.

A land may be covered with historic trophies . . . with universities and with libraries; the people may be civilised and ingenious; the country may even be famous in the annals and actions of the world, but if the population every ten years decreases, and the stature of the race every ten years diminishes, the history of that country will soon be the history of the past.

(Benjamin Disraeli, speech at Manchester, April 1872)

Now what is the feeling upon these subjects of the Liberal Party? A leading member denounced them the other day as 'the policy of sewage'.

Well it may be the policy of sewage to a Liberal member of Parliament. But to one of the labouring multitude of England, who has found fever always to be one of the inmates of his household . . . it is a question of life and death.

(Benjamin Disraeli, speech at Crystal Palace, June 1872)

[2]

1 How did Gladstone *increase the well-being of the working classes* by (i) budgetary and trade policies, (ii) encouragement of thrift? Why did the mass of the working classes not benefit from these policies?

2 What was meant by *the adulteration of food*? How did Disraeli's Government deal with this problem?

3 Why was *fever always . . . one of the inmates* of millions of homes?

4 Why was *the policy of sewage* dependent on strong and active local government? Which city particularly benefited from legislation passed by Disraeli's Government?

3 The aims of Tory democracy

Gentlemen, some years ago the Tory party experienced a great overthrow. I am here to admit that in my opinion it was deserved. A long course of power and prosperity had induced it to sink into a state of apathy and indifference. Instead of the principles professed by Mr. Pitt and Lord Grenville, the Tory system had degenerated into a policy which found an adequate basis on the principles of exclusiveness and restriction. Gentlemen, the Tory party, unless it is a national party is nothing. It is not a confederacy of nobles, it is not a democratic multitude; it is a party formed from all the numerous classes in the realm.

Now, I have always been of opinion that the Tory party has three great objects. The first is to maintain the institutions of the country. The discontent upon the subject of the representation . . . was terminated by the Act of Parliament Reform of 1867–68. That Act was founded on a confidence that the great body of the people of this country were 'Conservative'. When I say 'Conservative', I use the word in its purest and loftiest sense. I mean that the people of England and especially the working classes of England, are proud of belonging to a great country . . . that they believe, on the whole, that the greatness and the empire of England are to be attributed to the ancient institutions of the land.

Gentlemen, there is another and second great object of the Tory party—to uphold the Empire of England . . . Another great object of the Tory party is the elevation of the condition of the people . . .

(Disraeli's speech at Crystal Palace, June 1872)

[3]

1 Over which issue had *the Tory party experienced a great overthrow* earlier in the century?

2 How far had Peel changed the Tories from being a *confederacy of nobles*? How had he won the support of the middle classes by his policies after 1841? What attitude had Disraeli taken towards Peel at that time? Why?

3 Name three of *the institutions of the country* which Disraeli was anxious to maintain. Say, briefly, why he wished to do so.

4 What did Disraeli mean by saying that the Tory party was *a national party*? How far could that claim have been made by (i) Gladstone for the Liberals, and (ii) Salisbury for the Tories after Disraeli's death? Why?

5 After studying items 2 and 3 make a summary of the issues which Disraeli considered to be important.

4 The Artisans' Dwelling Act, 1875

Various portions of many cities and boroughs are so built, and the buildings thereon are so densely inhabited, as to be highly injurious to the moral and physical welfare of the inhabitants. There are in such cities and boroughs a great number of houses which, by reason of the want of air or of proper conveniences, are unfit for human habitation. Fevers and diseases are constantly generated there, causing death and loss of health, not only in the courts and alleys but also in other parts of such cities and boroughs;

Owing to the fact that such houses are the property of several owners, it is not in the power of any one owner to make such alterations as are necessary for the public health;

Many such houses should be pulled down, and such portions of the said cities and boroughs should be reconstructed. Be it enacted,

Where an official representation is made to the local Authority that any houses within a certain area are unfit for human habitation, or that diseases have been from time to time prevalent in a certain area . . . the local Authority shall pass a resolution to the effect that such area is an unhealthy area, and that an improvement scheme ought to be made in respect of such area, and after passing such a resolution shall forthwith proceed to make a scheme for the improvement of such area.

[4]
1 Why were so many houses *unfit for human habitation*? How would (i) house owners, and (ii) tenants, have explained the lack of amenities in these houses?
2 What causes of high death rate are (i) mentioned in, and (ii) omitted from this extract?
3 Why was *any one owner* unable to make improvements in these conditions?
4 How did this Act differ in scope from the Torrens Act of 1868?
5 Why were many councils unwilling to use the powers available under this Act? Why were they unable to ignore the terms of the Public Health Act of 1875? What official had to be appointed under the terms of that Act?

5 A blaze of triumph

A BLAZE OF TRIUMPH!

[5]
1 Why had Britain almost gone to war with Russia in 1877? Why was Britain opposed to the expansion of Russian influence in the Balkans?
2 Britain took possession of Cyprus in 1878. To whom had it belonged before that date? Why did Britain take Cyprus? Name two other British possessions which helped make the Mediterranean a British 'lake'.
3 Which nation was represented by the figure on Disraeli's back? In what ways did Britain support Turkey in 1878? How did Turkey reward that support in 1914?
4 What slogan did Disraeli coin to describe his success? How did Gladstone use this success against Disraeli in 1879? How, in 1880, did the electorate show that they had turned against Disraeli?

6 Gladstone on the Bulgarian horrors

We know that there have been perpetrated under the authority of a Government to which we have been giving the strongest support, outrages so vast in scale as to exceed all modern example. These are the Bulgarian horrors. What can be done to punish, or to brand, or to prevent these?

Twenty years ago, France and England determined to try a great experiment in remodelling the administrative system of Turkey, with the hope of curing its intolerable vices, and of making good its not less intolerable deficiencies. A vast expenditure of French and English life and treasure gave to Turkey twenty years of repose. The insurrections of 1875 have disclosed the total failure of the Porte to fulfil the engagements which she had contracted. Even these miserable insurrections, she had not the ability to put down. A lurid glare is thrown over the whole case by the Bulgarian horrors.

I entreat my countrymen to require and insist that our Government, which has been working in one direction, shall work in the other, and shall apply all its vigour to concur with the other states of Europe in obtaining the extinction of the Turkish executive power in Bulgaria. Let the Turks now carry away their abuses in the only possible manner, namely by carrying off themselves, their Zaptiehs and their Mudirs, their Bimbashis and their Yuzbachis, their Kaimakams and their Pashas, one and all, bag and baggage.

(W. E. Gladstone, *The Bulgarian Horrors and the Question of the East*, 1876)

[6]
1 Which *Government* had been responsible for these *outrages*? How had Britain given support to that government in (i) 1839, (ii) 1854?
2 Which people first rose in rebellion in 1875? Why?
3 What did Gladstone want *our Government* to do? Why was it unwilling to do so?
4 Which foreign government did help the rebellious Christians? What success did it enjoy in the war?
5 What were the main aims of the Treaty of San Stefano which ended that war? Why did that Treaty annoy *our Government*?

7 Peace with honour

As soon as the packet which was bringing back the two English plenipotentiaries touched the pier at Dover, the Mayor and Corporation stepped on board to present the Premier with a congratulatory address. The Premier in making his acknowledgements, claimed to have brought back 'Peace with Honour' and demanded recognition for Lord Salisbury's share in this result as equal to his own.

Other addresses of welcome and congratulation followed, and Ministers proceeded by special train to London. The Charing Cross Station had been decorated in their honour, and was crowded with spectators who closely packed the tiers of seats which had been erected. The arrival of the Ministers was greeted with ringing cheers. They were received upon the platform by the Lord Mayor and Sheriffs, in their robes of office, and a distinguished company. Something of the air of a triumph was given to their progress along the crowded way to Downing Street. In response to the cheers of the throng Lord Beaconsfield appeared at a window and repeated the phrase which he had used at Dover.

(G. C. Thompson, *Public Opinion and Lord Beaconsfield*, 1886)

[7]
1 Who were *the two English plenipotentiaries*? From where were they returning?
2 Who was *the Premier*? By what name is he referred to in this extract? By what name is he better remembered in history?
3 What post did *Lord Salisbury* hold at this time? When and why did he later say that 'We had backed the wrong horse'?
4 What territorial gain had the two Ministers made for Britain when achieving *Peace with Honour*? How, in that *Peace*, had they blocked Russian ambitions?

8 Disraeli and the Suez Canal, 1875

I had heard that the Khedive's canal shares would pass into French hands. Many politicians in this country had always disliked the Suez Canal scheme; one result of which was that the property was nearly all French. About 86 per cent of the tonnage that passed through the Canal was British. The British merchant, was paying the dividends, the French public was receiving them. The consequence was that the canal dues were kept very high.

I asked Lord Derby to consider what the chances of ever getting the canal dues lowered would be if the whole of the property passed into the hands of the French. Then arose another question. What authority or what means had the Government for buying shares in a commercial company? Parliament was not sitting, and even if it was and the House of Commons were asked for this £4,000,000 'the gaff would be blown' to use Lord Derby's own phrase. [Laughter.] The French would immediately be on the qui vive.

Lord Rowton was sent by Mr. Disraeli to Baron Rothschild; although the Baron must have been rather staggered at being asked to supply four millions in a very few days without any security. [Laughter.] But the money was furnished. Not a whisper got out, nobody heard a word of what was going on, and there came a Friday when all England acclaimed the great achievement which would redound for ever to the honour of Mr. Disraeli.

(From a speech in honour of Frederick Greenwood, 8 April 1905)

9 Disraeli writes to Queen Victoria, 24 November 1875

It is just settled; you have it, Madam. The French Government has been out-generalled. They tried too much, offering loans at an usurious rate, and with conditions which would have virtually given them the government of Egypt.

The Khedive, in despair and disgust, offered your Majesty's Government to purchase his shares outright. He would never listen to such a proposition before.

Four millions sterling! and almost immediately. There was only one firm that could do it — Rothschilds. They behaved admirably; advanced the money at a low rate, and the entire interest of the Khedive is now yours, Madam.

10 Salisbury attacks the Radicals, 1883

Take another question—the housing of the poor in our large towns. I hope that it may be the privilege of the present generation to assuage a vast amount of human misery. But I see an inclination to turn men from the question of how to relieve those evils in order to get up a fight between the landowning class and the rest of the country. The Radical politician appears to approach every question in order to find out material for hounding on one class against another. I do not believe that this is progress. We have enormous difficulties to encounter; we

[8, 9]

1 When was the Suez Canal opened? Who was the architect in charge of its building? In what way was the *property . . . nearly all French?*

2 Why was the canal important to British industrialists and traders? Why had the canal helped the development of the steamship?

3 Why was the canal later called 'the lifeline of the Empire'?

4 Who was *the Khedive?* Why did he have shares in the Canal Company? Why did he want to sell them in 1875?

5 What *security* did Disraeli offer Rothschild? When had a Rothschild first become an MP? What part had Disraeli played in that event?

6 Why did the purchase of these shares lead to Gladstone's involvement in (i) an Egyptian War, and (ii) the death of General Gordon? How far did these events lead to Britain taking control of the government of Egypt?

have a great population; the sources of prosperity are not flowing so abundantly as in the past, and the opportunities of industry are not numerous, and, therefore, the means of keeping the people from great suffering are engaging the minds of political men at the present time. They are no true friends of progress who persuade you that these objects are to be reached by generating quarrels.

(Speech of the Marquis of Salisbury, Reading, 30 October 1883)

11 Salisbury on taxation, trade and Empire, 1885

I want to point out to you the fundamental differences between the Conservative and the Radical proposals. The Conservative desire is so to manage affairs as to remove all restrictions, so as to give the necessary stimulus to industry, that you shall advance forward to conquer new realms of industry yet uninvaded, that you shall obtain the entry to markets that are now closed to you—that new markets shall be found for you; that, in short, the well-being of the working man shall be obtained by providing him with fresh material for his industry. The Conservative points the working man 'forward', to obtain wealth which is yet uncreated. The Radical turns his eyes backward, does not tell him to create new sources of wealth, but says that the wealth which has already been obtained is badly divided . . . and that the real remedy is to turn back and fight among yourselves for the wealth that has already been obtained.

(Speech of the Marquis of Salisbury, London, 4 November 1885)

12 Athwart the course

ATHWART THE COURSE.

R-ND-LPH CH-RCH-LL (an aggravating Boy). "IN THE WAY AGAIN! 'OORAY!!"

[10, 11]
1 Why were the poor able to afford only a low rent? How did this affect the quality of their housing? How has this problem been overcome in this century?
2 Name two leading Radical politicians of 1883. How did Radicals propose to force the landowning class to *relieve those evils*?
3 Why were the *sources of prosperity . . . not flowing so abundantly as in the past*? How had this been shown in (i) the agricultural industry, (ii) the level of British imports, and (iii) the unemployment figures?
4 How far had Salisbury accepted the arguments of the Free Traders? What was surprising about this?
5 Which classes (i) supported, (ii) opposed Salisbury's views? How far were his views responsible for the emergence of the Labour Party at the end of the century?

[12]
1 This cartoon appeared in 1883. Who was in charge of the first eight-oared boat (labelled *Government*)?
2 How did Churchill make life difficult for that government over (i) the Bradlaugh case, (ii) Egypt 1881, (iii) Ireland 1881–2, (iv) Home Rule 1886?
3 Who was in charge of the opposition party in 1883? Why was Churchill's conduct an indirect attack on his leadership? Which of Churchill's supporters in 1883 became Prime Minister in 1902?
4 Churchill was anxious to inherit the 'mantle of Disraeli'. Why did this lead to a conflict with Salisbury, whose views are expressed in items 10 and 11?
5 What part did Churchill play in (i) the Election of 1885, (ii) the Salisbury Government 1886?

Topic 10 Depression and Tariff Reform

1 Agricultural depression, 1882

All the witnesses whom we have examined have agreed in ascribing [the depression] mainly to a succession of unfavourable seasons.

Next to unfavourable seasons, foreign competition is alleged to have produced the most injurious effect. The unprecedently large importations, chiefly from America, have, by lowering the prices of home produce, greatly increased agricultural depression.

If it had not been for the enormous competition from America, prices in bad seasons would necessarily have gone up, and English produce would have found compensation for deficient yield.

Amongst the causes which have tended to aggravate the existing agricultural depression a prominent place is assigned by witnesses to the pressures of local taxation. Although the amount of poor rates does not appear to be excessive, yet the imposition of new rates, and the increase of old rates, press very heavily upon the agricultural interest.

The effect of the Education Act has been referred to by several employers as seriously interfering with farm work. 'It may have benefited the labourers themselves, but it has taken the best labourers off the farm.'

(Report of the Royal Commission on Agriculture, 1882)

[1]
1 Explain why and how foreign competition contributed to the *agricultural depression*. Which produce came *chiefly from America*?
2 How did some farmers escape the full effects of foreign competition? How were they helped by the existence of the British railway network?
3 Why did the standard of living of the urban worker rise during this depression?
4 Which *rates* were rising at this time? Why?
5 Which particular requirement of the Education Act of 1880 upset farmers?

2 Britain's industrial decline

For no small part of the supplies of essential commodities we found ourselves, in August 1914, dependent upon Germany. An analysis of our trade with Germany in 1913 will abundantly repay examination. Apart from the textile trades, our exports of manufactures to Germany made a very poor showing as compared with our imports of manufactures from Germany. Even in the cotton trade our exports of fully manufactured goods to Germany were only about one-third in value of our imports from Germany of the same kind. Indeed, when we come to analyse the £27,000,000 of manufactures which we sent to Germany we see that they were very largely composed of cotton and woollen yarn and waste, these items accounting for nearly £12,000,000. [Imports] consisted of fully manufactured, or highly finished articles, ranging from chemicals to earthenware, from dyes to musical instruments, and from scientific apparatus to specialised machinery.

The inefficiency of the British industries is by no means exclusively due to the workers who have endeavoured to limit output, but also to the manufacturers and to the Government. British employers have been too conservative. They have neglected new processes and inventions, they have relied for success rather on cheap labour than on the utmost efficiency in organisation.

(Sir Leo Money MP, *The British Dominions Year Book*, 1918)

[2]
1 Why had Britain become *dependent upon Germany* for so many essential supplies? Why was this a matter of great concern in August 1914?
2 What was the main difference in the quality of *our exports to Germany* and *our imports from Germany*?
3 How do you explain *the inefficiency of the British industries*? Who was to blame for that inefficiency?
4 What general conclusions can you draw from this document about the condition of British industry?

3 The steamship and the farmer

The economical applications of science in the vast improvements of the railroads and the steamships have changed the whole system of commerce. The effect has been to destroy local markets and to consolidate all into one market—the world. If our landlords and farmers want to know the names of the two persons who have knocked out the bottom of our old agricultural system, I can tell them. Their names are Sir Henry Bessemer and Dr. Joule. The first by his improvements in steel, has altered profoundly the transportation of commodities by sea and by land; and the second by his discoveries of the mechanical equivalent of heat, has led to great economy of coal in compound engines. By these changes the United States, Canada, India and Russia have their corn crops brought to our doors. A small cube of coal which would pass through a ring the size of a shilling, when burned in the compound engine of a modern steamboat, would drive a ton of food and its proportion of the ship two miles on its way from a foreign port. This economy of coal has altered the whole situation. Not long since a steamer of 3,000 tons going on a long voyage might require 2,200 tons of coal, and carry only a limited cargo of 800 tons. Now, a modern steamer will take the same voyage with 800 tons of coal and carry a freight of 2,200 tons. While coal has thus been economised, human labour has been lessened. In 1870 it required 47 hands on board our steamships for every 1,000 tons capacity. Now [1887] only 28 are necessary.

(Lyon Playfair, *Subjects of Social Welfare*, 1887)

[3]
1 How did the development of railroads help (i) British farmers in 1846–70, (ii) American farmers after 1870?
2 How did Sir Henry Bessemer affect the development of the steel industry? Why did his work affect *the transportation of commodities*?
3 Why were compound engines more efficient than they had been? How did this affect the cost of transporting goods from the USA? What effect did this have on the price of food in Britain?
4 Why, in 1887, were most of the world's steamships (i) owned by British firms, and (ii) built in British yards?

CAUGHT NAPPING!

THERE WAS AN OLD LADY AS I'VE HEARD TELL, | SHE WENT TO MARKET ON A MARKET DAY | BY CAME A PEDLAR—GERMAN—AND STOUT,
SHE WENT TO MARKET HER GOODS FOR TO SELL, | AND SHE FELL ASLEEP ON THE WORLD'S HIGHWAY. | AND HE CUT HER PETTICOATS ALL ROUND ABOUT.'

Caught napping

4 Against Free Trade, 1881

Thirty years ago England had almost a monopoly of the manufacturing industries of the world. The world was obliged to buy from her. Well, that was thirty years ago; now France and America and Belgium have got machinery, our machinery and our workmen and our capital, and they are sending us a yearly increasing surplus that is driving our own goods out of our own markets; and every year they are more completely closing their markets to our goods.

Foreigners form their own opinions from their own observations. When they see industries dying out under Free Trade in England, and springing into vigorous life under Protection in France, Belgium, Germany and America; when they see the ruin of agriculture, the depression of all manufacturing industries, operatives emigrating, capitalists preferring investments in foreign countries to those of their own, the fluctuations in prices and wages, the marked depreciation in the quality of English goods, the moral stagnation of the masses; when they see that as our population increases, our means of employing and feeding them decreases, they do not look much further for arguments against Free Trade.

(Edward Sullivan, *Isolated Free Trade*, 1881)

5 History reverses itself

HISTORY REVERSES ITSELF;

OR, PAPA JOSEPH TAKING MASTER ARTHUR A PROTECTION WALK.

Papa Joseph. "COME ALONG, MASTER ARTHUR. *DO* STEP OUT!"
Master Arthur. "THAT'S ALL VERY WELL, BUT YOU KNOW I CANNOT GO AS FAST AS YOU DO."

[4]
1 Why did the industrial development of France, America, and Belgium benefit some British firms?
2 How did other nations acquire *our capital*? Why was Britain (i) able, (ii) willing to provide that capital? Who, in Britain (i) gained, (ii) lost from this overseas investment?
3 How and why were overseas countries *closing their markets to our goods*?
4 Why were foreign goods *driving our own goods out of our own markets*? How far was this due to (i) British government policy, (ii) the quality of foreign goods, (iii) wage rates paid in overseas countries?

[5]
1 Who was represented in the inset cartoon by (i) the taller figure, and (ii) the shorter figure? When had that 'walk' been taken?
2 Who were represented by the two people in the larger cartoon?
3 Why did this cartoon appear in 1903 and not before?
4 What fiscal proposals did the taller man have in mind for (i) British tariffs in general, (ii) duties on food, (iii) tariffs on British goods entering countries in the British Empire?
5 How were the divisions inside the Conservative Party over this issue made public in 1903?

6 The acquisition of Rhodesia, 1889

Colonial Office to Foreign Office, Downing Street. May 16, 1889

I am directed by Lord Knutsford to transmit to you correspondence between this Department and Lord Gifford, V.C., Chairman of the Exploring Company (Limited) about a company to be formed for developing the Bechuanaland Protectorate and the countries to the north.

I also enclose a letter from Mr. C. J. Rhodes, of the Cape Colony, and two other gentlemen, who, as representing the holders of Concession from Lo Bengula, state that they have arranged to co-operate in any such scheme as that proposed.

The example of the Imperial East African Company shows that such a body may to some considerable extent, relieve Her Majesty's Government from diplomatic difficulties and heavy expenditure. In Lord Knutsford's judgement such a company as that proposed for the Bechuanaland Protectorate, if well conducted, would render still more valuable assistance to Her Majesty's Government in South Africa.

Lord Knutsford would suggest, for Lord Salisbury's consideration, whether the company might include such portion of territory north of the Zambesi as it may be important to control with a view to the security of communications with the Shire and Lake Nyassa, and the protection of British missionary settlements.

[6]

1 Why was it felt necessary to form companies to develop trade with parts of Africa? Why were they described as chartered companies?
2 How and why did the Government encourage such companies?
3 What *Concession* had Rhodes won from Lo Bengula?
4 When and why did the failure of the East African Company lead to government intervention in Uganda and Kenya?
5 What part was played by Rhodes in the conflict with the Boers between 1890 and 1895?

7 Chamberlain and the British Empire

(a) I regard many of our colonies as being in the condition of undeveloped estates. Cases have already come to my knowledge of colonies which have been British Colonies perhaps for more than a hundred years in which up to the present time British rule has done absolutely nothing. I shall be prepared to consider very carefully myself any case which may occur in which by the judicious investment of British money those estates which belong to the British Crown may be developed for the benefit of their population and for the benefit of the greater population which is outside.

(Joseph Chamberlain, speech, 1895)

(b) It is only in such a policy of development that I can see any solution of those great social problems by which we are surrounded. Plenty of employment and a contented people go together. I am sorry to say that Great Britain has in many cases neglected this duty of a mother country very much to her own injury as well as that of the population under her care. I may submit to you, as I did to the House of Commons, what is in a certain sense a new policy. It is a great policy. It is indeed open to criticism, for you cannot undertake a policy of this kind without a certain amount of risk. But if the people of this country are not willing to invest some of their superfluous wealth in the development of their great estate, then I see no future for these countries, and it would have been better never to have gone there.

(Joseph Chamberlain, speech to West African Railways Deputation, 1895)

[7]

1 When did Chamberlain become Colonial Secretary? Who was Prime Minister at that time?
2 Who had originally provided the *investment of British money* required for the development of British colonies? How had that money been spent? What advantages did the Government offer the investors?
3 What changes did Chamberlain propose? Which parts of the Empire particularly benefited from this changed policy?
4 How did his proposals benefit *the greater population*?
5 What political risk was involved by the participation of *the British Crown* in the development of the Empire? How far was this minimised by a conference held in 1890? How far was the risk illustrated by (i) a crisis in the Sudan in 1898, and (ii) the Second Boer War which started in 1899?

8 Chamberlain and tariffs, 1903

Ladies and gentlemen, I am not afraid to come here to the home of Adam Smith and to combat free imports, and still less am I afraid to preach to you preference with our colonies. I do not regard this as a party meeting. I am no longer a party leader. What are our objects? They are two. In the first place, we all desire the maintenance and increase of the national strength and the prosperity of the United Kingdom. Then, in the second place, our object is, or should be, the realisation of the greatest ideal which has ever inspired statesmen in any country or in any age—the creation of an Empire such as the world has never seen.

I want to prepare you now, while there is time, for a struggle ... from which, if we emerge defeated, this country will lose its place, will no longer count among the great nations of the world. If you will compare your trade in 1872, thirty years ago, with the trade of 1902—the export trade—you will find that there has been a moderate increase of £22,000,000. That, I think, is something like 7½ per cent. Meanwhile, the population has increased 30 per cent. In the same time the increase in the United States of America was £110,000,000 and the increase in Germany was £56,000,000. In the United Kingdom our export trade has been practically stagnant for thirty years.

But now there is one thing which follows—that is, that our Imperial trade is absolutely essential to our prosperity at the present time. If that trade declines, or if it does not increase in proportion to our population and to the loss of trade with foreign countries, then we sink at once into a fifth-rate nation.

Now I have told you what you are to gain by preference. You will gain the retention and the increase of your customers. You will gain work for the enormous number of those who are now unemployed, you will pave the way for a firmer and more enduring union of the Empire. What will it cost? What do the colonies ask? They ask a preference on their particular products ... you must put a tax on food.

(Chamberlain in Glasgow, 6 October 1903)

[8]
1 Who was Adam Smith? What had he said about *free imports*?
2 Why was Chamberlain no longer a party leader? How did his policies affect (i) the Liberals in 1886, and (ii) the Conservatives in 1906?
3 How far was he justified in describing *our export trade* as *stagnant* compared to (i) changes in the British population, and (ii) the growth of American and German exports?
4 What was meant by *preference*? How would this have helped to increase *our Imperial trade*?
5 Which colonies asked for a tax on food? Why?

9 The Liberals oppose Chamberlain, 1906

During the last few weeks the walls of Birmingham have been covered with a poster ... that poster shows you a big loaf, bigger than any I have ever seen—I should think it must weigh about eight and twenty pounds. It shows you a small loaf, smaller than any I have ever seen—and which, I suppose, might weigh a few ounces. And it tickets one 'The Free Trade Loaf', and it tickets the little one 'The Zollverein Loaf'. The placard has no object other than to induce you to believe that if you adopt my policy of preference with the Colonies, it is this little bit of a loaf to which you and your families will be reduced. I have had the curiosity to enquire what would be the exact difference in the size of the loaf if the whole tax which I propose was met by a corresponding reduction in the size of the loaf ... (Mr. Chamberlain here produced two quartern loaves which he held aloft.) I do not know

[9]
1 Which party put up the poster? Why did it do so in Birmingham in particular?
2 Which opposition politician led the anti-Chamberlain campaign?
3 Explain *The Zollverein*. How far, if at all, was Chamberlain advocating such an arrangement?
4 Which *preferences with the Colonies* did Chamberlain want the Government to adopt? Why would this have led to an increased price for bread?

whether your eyes are better than mine, but it is, I think, a sporting question which is the big one and which is the little one. What is to be said of a cause which is supported by such dishonest representations?

(Chamberlain speaking in Birmingham, 1906)

10 Chinese slavery

THE WAR'S RESULT CHINESE LABOUR

Voice of TOMMY ATKINS
(from the shadow)
"Is THIS what we fought for?"

The Tory Government have permitted Chinese Labourers to be imported into the Transvaal, there to work in the mines under conditions which Mr. Seddon described as "SEMI-SLAVERY."

(from the MORNING LEADER)

11 Chamberlain on the 1906 Election result

Personally, I should place the reasons for defeat in the following order;
(1) General weariness of a Government which had practically been in power for 20 years, and had become stale, and the consequent apathy among its supporters.
(2) Objection, especially among the Dissenters, to the Education policy of the Government.
(3) The intense feelings aroused against the employment of Chinese labour.
(4) The fears of the Trade Unionists that their funds are endangered by a recent decision of the Court of Appeal.

(Quoted in J. L. Garvin and J. Amery, *Life of Joseph Chamberlain*, 1932–1969)

5 Why would *The Free Trade Loaf* have to be either larger or cheaper than *The Zollverein Loaf*? How far were Chamberlain's opponents *dishonest*?

[10]
1 To which *war* does the poster refer? Why had Britain initially done badly in that war? Name two army leaders who led the British to ultimate victory.
2 How had that war helped *The Tory Government* to win the 1900 Election?
3 What effect had the war had on the unity of the Liberal Opposition in 1899?
4 Explain *Chinese labour*. How far did this system deserve to be described as *semi-slavery*?

[11]
1 When and why had Chamberlain resigned from the Government? Which leading member of that Government resigned in opposition to Chamberlain's proposals on Tariff Reform?
2 Explain *practically*, and say when, during the previous 20 years, the Conservatives had not been *in power*.
3 Explain *Dissenters*. Why were they opposed to *the Education policy of the Government*? How had that policy helped to unite the Liberal Party?
4 What *recent decision of the Court of Appeal* annoyed trade unionists? How did that decision affect the numbers of unions joining the Labour Representation Committee?

Topic 11 A Restless and Violent Society

1 The housing of the poor, 1883

You have to penetrate courts reeking with poisonous gases arising from the accumulations of sewage and refuse; courts, many of them never visited by a breath of fresh air. You have to ascend rotten staircases, grope your way along dark passages swarming with vermin. Then you gain admittance to the dens in which these thousands of beings herd together. Eight feet square—that is about the average size of very many of these rooms. Walls and ceilings are black with the accretions of filth which have gathered upon them. A window is half stuffed with rags or covered by boards to keep out wind and rain; you look out upon the roofs and ledges of lower tenements, and discover that the sickly air which finds its way into the room has to pass over the putrefying carcasses of dead cats or birds. As to furniture—you may perchance discover a broken chair, the tottering relics of an old bedstead or the mere fragment of a table; but more commonly you will find rude substitutes for these things in the shape of rough boards resting upon bricks, an old hamper or box turned upside down, or more frequently still, nothing but rubbish and rags

(Rev. Andrew Mearns, *The Bitter Cry of Outcast London*, 1883)

[1]
1 How had (i) Gladstone, and (ii) Disraeli tried to deal with the problem of slum housing?
2 Why were house builders unable to provide adequate housing at rents which the low paid could afford?
3 How did the high birth rate of the nineteenth century affect the housing problem?
4 What did (i) Sir Titus Salt, (ii) Octavia Hill, (iii) Ebenezer Howard do to improve housing conditions? Why was their work of little value to the majority of the badly housed?

2 Rowntree on the working poor, 1900

The wage for a labourer in York is from 18s to 21s; the minimum expenditure necessary to maintain in a state of physical efficiency a family of two adults and three children is 21s 8d, or, if there are four children, 26s.

The wages are insufficient to provide food, shelter and clothing adequate to maintain in a state of bare physical efficiency, even if the diet is less generous than that allowed in the Workhouse.

And let us clearly understand what 'merely physical efficiency' means. A family living upon the scale must never spend a penny on railway or omnibus; never go into the country unless they walk; never purchase a halfpenny paper or buy a ticket for a popular concert; never write letters to absent children, for they cannot afford the postage. They cannot save, join sick club or Trade Union; they cannot pay the subscriptions. The children have no pocket money. The father must not drink or smoke. The mother must never buy pretty clothes for herself or her children. Finally, the wage-earner must never be absent from his work for a single day.

If any of these conditions are broken, the extra expenditure is met, and can only be met, by limiting the diet.

(Seebohm Rowntree, *Poverty, a Study in Town Life*, 1902)

[2]
1 Why did Rowntree undertake a study of town life? How far was he influenced by the work of Charles Booth? Why did he concentrate on York?
2 What major cause of poverty was Rowntree describing in this extract? Give five other reasons why a family's income might be insufficient to provide food, shelter and clothing.
3 Why was the unskilled wage-earner likely to be absent from his work because of sickness?
4 How far does this extract explain the attitudes of the New Unions towards political activity? Why did the members of the older craft unions not share this attitude in 1900?

3 Shaftesbury opposes subsidised housing

If the State is to be summoned to provide houses for the labouring classes at nominal rents, it will, while doing something for their physical condition, destroy their moral energies. It will be an official proclamation that, without any efforts of their own, certain people shall enjoy many good things at the expense of others. The State is bound to give every facility by law, but the work itself should be founded . . . on voluntary effort.

Should private bounty be insufficient it might then be necessary for the Government to use State money for the improvement of the conditions of some of the labouring classes by placing them in new homes at subsidised rents.

The mischief of it would be very serious. It would give great discouragement to the spirit of thrift now rising among the people. The wise and considerate measures to give facilities for the investment of savings, specially those introduced at the Post Office, are greatly changing the character of the English nation, generally regarded, hitherto, as that of the most wasteful in Europe. But much of the old spirit still remains. 'My money is mine, and I've a right to spend it as I like, and if the worst comes to the worst, there's the workhouse.' This sentiment is still the sentiment of thousands in this country; nor will it be modified by the hints, given in speeches and pamphlets, of State benevolence. It is a melancholy system that tends to debase a large mass of the people to the condition of a nursery, where the children look to the father and mother, and do nothing for themselves.

(The Earl of Shaftesbury in *The Nineteenth Century*, 1883)

[3]

1 What had Shaftesbury done to improve conditions for (i) factory workers, (ii) climbing boys? Why did this give added significance to this article?

2 How might *State money* be used to subsidise the rents of the *houses of the labouring classes*? Why did (i) the builders, and (ii) the badly housed need such a system of subsidies?

3 Why did Shaftesbury refer only to *certain people*? How had some working class people acquired their own homes? Why were others able to afford the rents for decent housing?

4 Which Radical Liberal politician was advocating increased government spending on social reform? Do you think that such spending destroys people's *moral energies*? Why?

Children of the poor

4 Unemployed rioters, 1887

Just before three o'clock, other bodies of men came, with banners flying and bands playing, out to the green. They were greeted with loud cheers. I noticed the banners of the East Finsbury Radical Club and of the Clerkenwell branch of the Social Democratic Federation. The banner of the latter association bore the words 'Educate, Agitate, Organise'.

When the procession reached the Bloomsbury end of St. Martin's Lane, the police, mounted and on foot, charged in among the people, striking indiscriminately in all directions. At four o'clock the processions from Peckham, Bermondsey, Deptford and Battersea made their appearance at the Westminster end of the bridge . . . and for these the police made. During the melee, the police freely used their weapons, and the people, who were armed with iron bars, pokers, gas-pipes and short sticks, and even knives, resisted them in a most determined manner. Several arrests were in this instance made by the police, their chief captures being those of Mr. C. Graham, MP, and Mr. John Burns, who were carried into the middle of the square, and kept in custody there for some little time.

(*Reynolds' News*, 20 November 1887)

[4]

1 Who founded *the Social Democratic Federation*? What were the main aims of this society?

2 Why was there more unemployment in the 1880s than there had been in the 1860s?

3 What part did John Burns play in (i) the London Dockers' Strike, 1889, (ii) the formation of the Labour Party 1893–1900, (iii) the Liberal Government 1906?

4 Why were the unemployed dissatisfied with the existing political system? Which Society formed in the 1880s argued for an evolutionary change? Why did some people fear that there would be a revolutionary change?

Trafalgar Square riots

5 Looking for work, 1890

I went down to the riverside at Shadwell. No work was to be had there. Then I called at another place in Limehouse. No hands wanted. So I looked in at home and got two slices of bread in paper and walked eight miles to a cooper's yard in Tottenham. All in vain. I dragged myself back to Clerkenwell. Still no luck. Then I turned towards home in despair. By the time I reached Stepney I was dead beat, so I called at a friend's in Commercial Road for a little rest. They gave me some Irish stew and twopence to ride home. I managed to walk home and gave the twopence to my wife.

A man who is out of work for long nearly always degenerates. For example if a decent fellow falls out in October and fails to get a job by say March he loses his anxiety to work. The exposure, the insufficient food, his half-starved condition have such a deteriorating effect upon him that he becomes indifferent whether he gets work or not. He thus passes from the unemployed state to the unemployable state. It ought to be the duty of the nation to see that a man does not become degenerate.

(G. Haw, *From Workhouse to Westminster: The Life Story of Will Crooks*, 1907)

[5]
1 Why was work at *the riverside at Shadwell* (i) irregular, (ii) badly paid?
2 Why did many workers lose their jobs between October and March? Why was this described as seasonal unemployment? Name three trades which suffered from this type of unemployment.
3 What help, if any, might unemployed workmen get from the State in the 1890s? How might Crooks have been helped by a system of Labour Exchanges?
4 How did the Liberal Government, 1906–14, help the unemployed?

6 The Triple Alliance, 1914

One result of the industrial unrest of recent years is the Triple Alliance.

At the Miners' Annual Conference in 1913, a resolution was passed, 'That the Executive Committee of the Miners' Federation approach the Executive Committee of other big Trade Unions with a view to co-operative action.'

The miners had a joint meeting with the representatives of the two industries most comparable to their own—railways and transport.

The three bodies have much in common. Their membership is considerable, the miners number 800,000, the railwaymen 270,000 and the transport workers 260,000. The miners have done much fighting; the railwaymen have come through struggles similar to our own; and the transport workers are famed for their fighting spirit and fighting qualities. But a great deal of suffering and privation has been caused. A strike on the railway system affects the miners and the transport workers. When the miners struck in 1912 the cost to the railwaymen alone was about £94,000.

The new body is not to be a rival to any other. Nor is it to be sectional in any sense. There is no suggestion that if one section of the miners determines to strike they will receive the assistance of the new alliance. Action is to be confined to joint national action. The predominant idea is that each of these great fighting organisations, before embarking upon any big movement, either defensive or aggressive, should formulate its programme, submit it to the others, and that upon joint proposals action should then be taken.

It will be wise, indeed essential, to have the working agreement ready for the days of peace after the war. It is then that we may expect an attack on Labour by the employers.

(Robert Smillie, *The Labour Year Book*, 1916)

[6]
1 How did (i) rising unemployment, (ii) changes in the cost of living, (iii) the development of New Unionism, and (iv) rising expectations among the working class contribute to *the industrial unrest of recent years*?
2 Why and how would a strike in the railway industry lead to unemployment among miners and transport workers?
3 Why did a miners' strike in 1912 cost the railwaymen £94,000?
4 What was meant by *joint proposals*? How far does this help to explain the origins of the General Strike of 1926?

7 The suffragettes, 1905

The country was on the eve of a general election in which the Liberals hoped to be returned to power. The Liberal candidates went to the country with promises of reform in every possible direction. We determined to address ourselves to those men who were likely to be in the Liberal Cabinet, demanding to know whether their reforms were going to include justice to women.

We laid our plans to begin this work at a great meeting to be held in the Free Trade Hall, Manchester, with Sir Edward Grey as the principal speaker. Annie Kenney and my daughter Christabel were charged with the mission of questioning Sir Edward Grey. They sat quietly through the meeting, at the close of which questions were invited. Several questions were asked by men and were courteously answered. Then Annie Kenney arose and asked: 'If the Liberal party is returned to power, will they take steps to give votes for women?' At the same time Christabel held aloft the little banner that everyone in the hall might understand the nature of the question. Sir Edward Grey returned no answer to Annie's question, and the men sitting near her forced her rudely to her seat, while a steward pressed his hat over her face.

Annie Kenney stood up in her chair and cried out over the noise of shuffling feet and murmurs of conversation: 'Will the Liberal Government give votes to women?' Then the audience became a mob. They howled, they shouted and roared, shaking their fists fiercely at the woman who dared to intrude her question into a man's meeting. Flung into the streets, the two girls staggered to their feet and began to address the crowds. Within five minutes they were arrested on a charge of obstruction and, in Christabel's case, of assaulting the police. Both were summonsed to appear next morning in a police court, where, after a trial which was a mere farce, Annie Kenney was sentenced to pay a fine of five shillings, with an alternative of three days in prison, and Christabel Pankhurst was given a fine of ten shillings or a jail sentence of one week. Both girls promptly chose the prison sentence.

(Emmeline Pankhurst, *My Own Story*, 1924)

8 Irish Home Rule

The national demand is that the government of every purely Irish affair shall be controlled by the public opinion of Ireland alone. We demand this self-government as a right. For us the Act of Union has no binding force. We regard it as a great criminal act of usurpation, carried by violence and by fraud.

Resistance to the Act of Union will always remain a sacred duty . . . and we declare that no ameliorative reforms, no number of Land Acts, or Labourers Acts, or Education Acts, can ever satisfy Ireland until Irish laws are made and administered upon Irish soil by Irishmen.

But our claim to self-government does not rest solely upon historic right. It rests also upon the failure of the British government in Ireland for the last hundred years. Take the test of population. While in every civilised country in Europe the population has increased . . . in Ireland,

[7]

1 How did the campaign of the suffragettes differ from campaigns of other suffrage societies? How did Mrs Pankhurst justify the difference?

2 Why did they launch a major campaign in 1905? Why did they pay more attention to members of a future Liberal Cabinet than to the mass of Liberal candidates? Why did they not bother about the Conservative candidates?

3 Why did *both girls promptly* choose *the prison sentence*? Why was the Government forced to pass the Cat-and-Mouse Act to deal with suffragette prisoners?

4 What did Miss Emily Davison do to attract attention to the suffragettes' campaign?

5 When did women (i) first get the vote, (ii) get the vote on equal terms with men?

[8]

1 When was *the Act of Union* passed? How had it affected the system of government for Ireland? Why did Catholics in particular think it was a fraud when it was passed?

2 Why had the population of Ireland declined in the nineteenth century while that of Great Britain had risen?

3 Which organisations had led *insurrections* in (i) 1848, (ii) 1865?

4 How were Irish farmers affected by the rise in imports of food from America?

5 Why did the Irish expect to get more sympathy from the Liberals than they had got from the Conservatives before 1906? Why was the Liberal Government able to ignore the demands of Irish MPs between 1900 and 1909? Why was the Government forced to pay attention to those demands in 1910?

in the last sixty years, it has diminished by one-half. Take the test of civil liberty. There has been a Coercion Act for every year since the Union was passed, and there is today in existence a law which enables the Lord Lieutenant by a stroke of the pen, to suspend trial by jury, personal liberty, freedom of discussion, and the right to public meeting all over Ireland.

Take the test of the contentment of the people. There have been since the Union three insurrections, all of them suppressed in blood. Take the test of the prosperity of Ireland . . . it is the history of constantly-recurring famines every few years over a large portion of the west and north-west seaboard of the country. Take the question of industrial development. A history of industries deliberately suppressed by British Acts of Parliament, and not one finger lifted in the last hundred years to advance industrial prosperity. Now such a record as that cries aloud for vengeance.

(John Redmond's speech, Dublin, 4 September 1907)

9 Ulster prepares to fight, 1912–1914

While I had still in the party a position of less responsibility than that which I have now, I said that if an attempt was made without the clearly expressed will of the people of this country, and as part of a corrupt Parliamentary bargain, to deprive these men of their birth-right, they would be justified in resisting by all means in their power, including force. I can imagine no length of resistance to which Ulster will go in which I shall not be ready to support them and in which they will not be supported by the overwhelming majority of the British people.

(Bonar Law, speech at Blenheim, 27 July 1912)

10 The Ulster Covenant, 1912

Being convinced that Home Rule would be disastrous to the material well-being of Ulster, subversive of our civil and religious freedom, and perilous to the unity of the Empire, we men of Ulster, humbly relying on the God whom our fathers in days of stress and trial confidently trusted, do hereby pledge ourselves in solemn Covenant to stand by one another in defending for ourselves and our children our cherished possession of equal citizenship in the United Kingdom, and in using all means which may be found necessary to defeat the present conspiracy to set up a new Home Rule Parliament in Ireland. And in the event of such a Parliament being forced upon us, we further solemnly and mutually pledge ourselves to refuse to recognise its authority. In sure confidence that God will defend the right we hereto subscribe our names . . . God Save the King.

(The Ulster Covenant, 1912)

[9]
1 What position did Bonar Law have in *the party* in 1912? When had he obtained that position? Whom had he succeeded?
2 Between whom had there been *a corrupt Parliamentary bargain* in 1910? What did that bargain say about (i) the future government of Ireland, (ii) the power of the House of Lords?
3 Why did the Liberals claim that *the people of this country* had *clearly expressed* their support for Home Rule in 1910? Why could Law claim that this was not true?
4 How far was Bonar Law responsible for the climate of opinion which encouraged 'the Curragh Mutiny'? What effect did this have on the policy of the Liberal Government towards Ulster?

[10]
1 Who, in 1886, had coined the slogan 'Ulster will fight and Ulster will be right'?
2 How different was Ulster from the rest of Ireland as regards (i) religion, and (ii) economic development?
3 Which Anglo-Irish MP organised the signing of the *Ulster Covenant*? What office had he held in the Conservative Government up until 1905?
4 Why was this Covenant published in 1912 and not, for example, in 1910?
5 How did the people of Ulster prepare to defend *ourselves and our children*? How did Redmond's followers react? Why did many people think that there would be a civil war in Ireland? Why was this danger greater in 1914? How was the Irish question affected by the outbreak of war in 1914?

Topic 12 The Labour Party, 1867–1914

1 The Vote, 1867

In the House of Commons there are 658 members, whose business it is to make the laws under which the whole of the people of all classes live. Every one of the 658 belongs to the middle and upper classes. Labour has not one direct representative—there is not in the House of Commons ONE MAN whose life has been spent in the workshop in intimate daily experience of the working man's trials. Working men! We call on you as a paramount and pressing duty, to return qualified men of your own to Parliament.

(Address of the Labour Representation League to the Working Men Electors of the United Kingdom, 1871)

2 The New Unionism, 1889

From the Dock Strike of 1889, the present day organisation of the wage-earners took its rise. It marked the beginning of that close alliance in thought and purpose between the Trade Union Movement and the Socialist Movement which produced in due time the Labour Party. Trade Unionism among the general workers was an absolute weakling, regarded as an illegitimate offspring, and treated like one by the respectable Trade Unionism of the skilled crafts and trades. To set our Union on its feet and to win the respect of the craft Unions, we had to demonstrate the strength of our purpose in actual warfare with the employers. The Dock Strike was a test, not only of intelligence and will on our part, but of the ability to seize opportunities as they arose, to evoke and to make use of public sympathy as one of the weapons of our warfare.

(Ben Tillett, *Memories and Reflections*, 1931)

3 The Fabians

(a) All students of society realize that important organic changes can only be (1) democratic, and thus acceptable to a majority; (2) gradual, and thus causing no dislocation; (3) not regarded as immoral by the mass of the people; (4) in this country, at any rate, constitutional and peaceful. Socialists may therefore be quite at one with Radicals in their political methods. There is every day a wider concensus that the inevitable outcome of Democracy is the control by the people themselves of the main instruments of wealth production. The economic side of the democratic ideal is, in fact, Socialism itself.

(S. Webb, *Fabian Essays*, 1889)

[1]
1 Why was it possible for working men to be elected to Parliament in 1871? When had the middle classes obtained that privilege?
2 What financial considerations prevented working men from (i) standing as candidates in elections, (ii) wanting to become MPs? Why did these considerations not affect the middle and upper classes?
3 How was the possibility of having working-class MPs affected by Acts passed in (i) 1872, (ii) 1884, (iii) 1911?

[2]
1 Who was Ben Tillett? What part did he play in *the Dock Strike of 1889*? To which political society did he belong at that time?
2 Name three societies of *the Socialist Movement*. Which was (i) the most socialist, (ii) the most influential in the formation of the Labour Party?
3 What were the main differences between the general unions and the craft unions as regards (i) *warfare*, (ii) self-help?
4 How was the revival of the *Trade Union Movement* indicated by the changed attitude of the TUC towards the Independent Labour Party between 1893 and 1900?

[3]
1 Why was the description *students of society* particularly suitable for the Fabians? Name three leading Fabians apart from Sidney and Beatrice Webb.

(*b*) Their tactics are to fight the Liberals, not as decided opponents, but to drive them on to Socialistic consequences; therefore to trick them, to permeate Liberalism with Socialism.

(Frederick Engels, writing in 1893)

4 A bit of a breeze

[4]

1 Which politician was represented by the organ grinder? When did he (i) become Prime Minister, (ii) lead his party to an electoral victory, (iii) retire?
2 Explain *Liberal Labour* on the blouse of the dancing girl.
3 What was *Independent* about Keir Hardie's Labour Party? When was that party founded?

2 Which word in the extract shows that the Fabians believed in evolution rather than revolution? How did Webb justify this approach to change?
3 Which clause in this extract foreshadowed the Labour Party's proposals on nationalisation?
4 Why did the Fabians concentrate their propaganda on the Liberals rather than Salisbury's Conservatives or some of the Socialist societies?

When did Hardie become an MP for the first time?
4 Explain the differences between the *Liberal Labour* and the *Independent Labour* parties as regards (i) their supporters, (ii) their ambitions.
5 Why was the independence of Hardie's party a threat to the party led by the organ grinder?

5 George Bernard Shaw on the power of the unions, 1893

Before the London Dock Strike [1889] the Trade Union organisation was limited to little more than half a million; even so it was richer, and more powerful and responsible for the condition of the Labour movement than any other body in the country. Since that time the establishment of a great number of unions in *formerly unrecognised trades* has trebled the numbers, increased the political power and responsibility of the Trade Union movement.

Attempts have been made by Socialists to establish societies to relieve the unions of their political duty, at a General Election the unions could put up 2,000 votes for one single voter of the most successful of their rivals.

The money difficulty does not exist for unions. A penny a week from every member of a trade union would produce £300,000. This shows how easily the larger unions alone could provide £30,000 to finance 50 candidates at £600 apiece.

Representation of the working classes at the General Election will depend on the trade unions not on *Socialist bodies*.

(George Bernard Shaw, *An open letter to the Trade Unions*, 1893)

[5]

1 Why were there only about half a million men enrolled in trade unions before 1889?
2 Name two *formerly unrecognised trades* which formed unions after the strike of 1889.
3 Why did candidates need to be financed? Why could unions afford to provide this financial help? How was this help affected by Acts passed in (i) 1911, and (ii) 1913?
4 Why, apart from financial aid, did the *representation of the working classes . . . depend on the trade unions*?
5 Shaw was a Fabian. How far did this letter represent a change in Fabian policy? Why did the results of *the General Election* lead Fabians to make this change?

6 Hardie appeals to the TUC, 1899

'That this congress . . . hereby instructs the Parliamentary Committee to invite the co-operation of all the co-operative, socialistic, trade union, and other working-class organisations to jointly co-operate on lines mutually agreed upon in convening a special congress of representation from such of the above-named organisations as may be willing to take part to devise ways and means for the securing the return of an increased number of Labour members to the next Parliament.'

He said the sooner the trade unionists recognised the fact that it was only by disassociating themselves from both the great political parties that they could obtain the balance of power, so that they might dictate their own terms to either Liberals or Conservatives, the better it would be for the interests of labour.

(Quoted in Philip Viscount Snowden, *An Autobiography*, 1934)

7 Pioneering days in Yorkshire

I joined my Trade Union towards the end of 1882. It was the old Weavers' Union, established in 1881. The contributions were nil. We paid for our cards and rules, and the funds were raised by a very slight monthly, quarterly or special levy.

As Leeds and District Secretary for the Union with a wage of five shillings a week I went into the 'hurly-burly' of Leeds Labour life.

I joined at once the Leeds Socialist Party. The membership was mixed but not large. The club was about a mile and a quarter from our house. I also joined the Leeds Trades Council in 1889. The Socialist Club folks were anti-Trades Council. It was at this club that I met Michael Davitt, William Thorne and many another old Labour reformer.

We younger folks wanted to lead the Trades Union movement out of the Liberal Party fold, and as the unions grew stronger the Socialist force grew stronger and a large number of Labour Clubs were formed, especially in the Industrial areas of the West Riding.

(Ben Turner, *About Myself*, 1930)

8 The birth of the Labour Party, 1900

The new movement did not begin auspiciously. At the end of the first year only 40 Trade Unions out of about 1200 then existing had affiliated, with a membership of 353,000. The great organisations of the miners and the textile workers stood aloof, looking on the new movement with suspicion and regarding it with undisguised hostility. The first Annual Conference was held in Manchester in February 1901; and I well remember the feeling of despondency which prevailed.

During the previous year [1900] a General Election had taken place. It came before the new Committee had had time to get into its work. The ILP had nine candidates in the field, and the Trade Unions four. Of these only two were successful—Keir Hardie at Merthyr and Mr. Richard Bell at Derby.

[6]

1 When had *this congress* met for the first time? When and why had it set up a *Parliamentary Committee*?

2 Why had this resolution been rejected in former years? How had the membership of the congress changed in the 1890s?

3 Which of *the great political parties* had the leaders of the congress supported? How was this continued support shown in the vote on this resolution in 1899?

4 When and where did *a special congress* take place? How many *Labour members* were elected into the next Parliament?

5 What name was given to the organisation set up at that *special congress*? Who was chosen as its secretary?

[7]

1 What were the main differences between *my Trade Union* and the older craft unions as regards (i) contributions, (ii) benefits? Why did the members of the New Trade Unions pay so little in contributions?

2 Which League did *Michael Davitt* form in 1879? Which union had *William Thorne* founded?

3 Which type of union *grew stronger* in the 1890s? Why did some craft unions become more militant during this period? Why did they also become more interested in the idea of a Labour Party?

[8]

1 Why did *the great organisations* feel that they did not need *the new movement* (i) politically, (ii) socially?

2 Why was the ILP unable to put many candidates *in the field*?

3 Why did the Labour Representation Committee have no funds in 1900–1? How did it raise funds later on? Why was

Keir Hardie was again the solitary independent Labour member of the new Parliament. His return raised a financial problem for the National Council of the ILP. There was no payment of members from the National Exchequer in those days. Hardie had no Trade Union behind him, and the newly formed Labour Representative Committee had no funds. The National Council set to work to raise a sum of £150 a year towards his support.

(Philip Viscount Snowden, *An Autobiography*, vol. 1, 1934)

the support of *the great organisations* essential in this respect?
4 Why did many of the great organisations join *the new movement* in 1901 and 1902? How far was this due to a failure on the part of the Balfour Government? Which Act was passed in 1906 to satisfy a demand of these organisations?

9 Unions join the Labour Party, 1901–1904

	Number of unions	Affiliated union membership	Unions affiliating on more than 10,000 members	LRC union membership as a proportion of TUC membership
Feb 1901–2	65	455,450		32%
Feb 1902–3	127	847,315	Boilermakers, Carpenters and Joiners, Engineers, Locomotive Engineers & Firemen	56%
Feb 1903–4	165	956,025	Bricklayers, Miners' Federation, Plumbers	67%

(Report on trade union affiliation to the LRC, 1900–6)

10 MacDonald and the electoral pact

(a) What would be the gain and the loss to the party at the General Election if a working arrangement were arrived at with the LRC?

The LRC can directly influence the votes of nearly a million men. They will have a fighting fund of £100,000. Their members are mainly men who have hitherto voted with the Liberal Party. Should they be advised to vote against Liberal candidates the Liberal Party would suffer defeat not only in those constituencies where LRC candidates fought, but also in almost every borough, and in many of the Divisions of Lancashire and Yorkshire. This would be the inevitable result of unfriendly action towards the LRC candidates. They would be defeated, but so also should we be defeated. If there be good-fellowship between us and the LRC the aspect of the future for both will be very bright and encouraging.

(F. Bealey quoted in the Bulletin of the Institute of Historical Research, vols 29–30, 1956)

(b) I have some reason to think that we may get them [the LRC] to a working agreement about constituencies, but before we do I should like the principle to be discussed. Bryce [a Liberal MP] used to be very stiff against any recognition of Labour candidates as distinct from Liberals. But it is a distinction we shall have to recognise and the sooner we can educate the constituencies the better—in my opinion.

(Herbert Gladstone in a letter to H. H. Asquith, 8 February 1903)

[9, 10]
1 Why was Asquith known as a Liberal Imperialist in 1903? What office was he to hold in (i) 1906, (ii) 1909?
2 How had some Liberals favoured some Labour candidates in certain constituencies? Which Labour leader first advocated that Labour candidates should be *distinct from Liberals*? When and why did he first take this stand?
3 What did the Liberals fear would happen if there was no *working arrangement*?
4 Name three major issues on which, in 1903, the Liberals and the Labour Representation Committee were united in hostility to the Government.
5 Which leader of the LRC arranged the pact in 1903? What links had he had with the Liberals in the past?

11 Sweated labour

[11]
1 Why were some women and children willing to undertake this work in the home?
2 Why did employers use this 'outwork' rather than bring their workpeople into a factory? Why were they able to pay very low wages?
3 What dangers were there to people's health in work of this sort?
4 Why were these homeworkers not controlled by existing Factory Acts?
5 How did the Liberal Government (1906–14) try to improve the conditions for these workers?

12 Tom Mann wants a more revolutionary movement, 1910

After our visit to Paris, Guy Bowman and I, with the support of a few representative trade unionists, decided to organize in Britain on lines similar to those which had been adopted by the French comrades . . . We published a small monthly called *The Industrial Syndicalist*. The first issue appeared in July 1910 . . . In July 1910, I wrote stating the Syndicalist case on broad general lines.

What is called for? What will have to be the essential conditions for the success of such a movement?

That it should be avowedly and clearly revolutionary in aim and method.

Revolutionary in aim because it will be out for the abolition of the wages system, and for securing to the workers the full fruits of their labour, thereby seeking to change the system of society from Capitalist to Socialist.

Revolutionary in method, because it will refuse to enter into any long agreements with the masters, whether with legal or State backing, or merely voluntarily; and because it will seize every chance of fighting for the general betterment.

Does this mean that we should become anti-political? Certainly not.

Let the politicians do as much as they can, and the chances are that, once there is an economic fighting force in the country ready to back them up by action, they will actually be able to do what would now be hopeless for them to attempt to do.

The workers should realize that it is the men who manipulate the tools and machinery who are the possessors of the necessary power to

[12]
1 What part did Tom Mann play in the Dockers' Strike, 1889?
2 What does this extract tell you about the aims of the Syndicalists?
3 What evidence is there in this extract that Mann and others were dissatisfied with the progress that had been made by the Labour movement by 1910?
4 Why did the development of Syndicalism frighten employers and other middle-class people?

achieve something tangible, and they will succeed just in proportion as they agree to apply concerted action.

The curse of capitalism consists in this—that a handful of capitalists can compel hundreds of thousands of workers to work in such manner and for such wage as will please the capitalists. But this again is solely because of the inability of workers to agree upon a common plan of action. The hour the workers agree and act, they become all-powerful. We can settle the capitalists' strike-breaking power once for all. We shall have no need to plead with parliamentarians to be good enough to reduce hours as the workers have been doing for a full twenty years without result. We shall be able to do this for ourselves, and there will be no power on earth to stop us.'

(Tom Mann, *Memoirs*, 1923)

13 A stormy meeting, August 1914

Hardie had yet another ordeal to pass through, and he resolved to face it at once before going home to the quietness of Cumnock. He had to see his constituents. On August 6th he spoke in Aberdare. What happened there had best be described by one who was present. 'As soon as the hall began to fill it was obvious that a large hostile element was present. The Chairman spoke without interruption, but as soon as he called on Hardie the uproar commenced. A well organised body of men had taken up a strong position near the back of the hall. They were the members of the Conservative and the Liberal Clubs who had always hated Hardie. Their opportunity had come at last. 'God Save the King' and 'Rule Britannia' were sung lustily, and the clang of a bell could be heard amongst the general pandemonium. Hardie continued to speak for about half an hour utterly undaunted by the noise, but his voice could not be heard further than the front seats. Once or twice a few scraps of phrases could be heard amidst the din. He was heard to refer to the German workers as good, kind-natured people and the noise drowned the rest. At last he sat down. A small body of comrades closed round Hardie. There was a rush near the door but the street was reached safely. The crowd surged down the side street, but in the main street it began to get less. But several hundred men followed us up the main street singing their jingo songs. Hardie was unperturbed. He walked straight on with his head erect, not deigning to look either to the right or to the left. He was staying with Matt Lewis, the school teacher, secretary of the local Labour Party . . . Hardie sat down in the armchair by the fire and lit his pipe. He was silent for a time staring into the fire. Then he joined in the conversation but did not talk so much as usual. I had to catch the nine o'clock train down the valley. He shook hands, and said, 'I understand what Christ suffered in Gethsemane as well as any man living'.

(William Stewart, *J. Keir Hardie*, 1921)

[13]
1 Of which constituency was Hardie the MP in 1914?
2 Why was he opposed to British participation in the war in August 1914? What arrangement did he think he had made with the German workers and with the leaders of the French workers?
3 What was the significance of the *jingo songs*? Which famous poet wrote 'jingo' poetry in 1914?
4 Why were many trade union members of the Labour Party so opposed to Hardie's attitude towards the war?
5 What attitude was taken towards the war by (i) Ramsay MacDonald, (ii) Arthur Henderson?
6 What was the effect of the war on the Liberal Party?

Topic 13 The Liberals, 1906–1914

1 Old Liberalism and new

What is the work still awaiting the Liberal Party in this country? It is to establish complete religious equality in our institutions. There is no religious equality as long as one sect whose dogmas, in Wales, are repudiated by the vast majority of the people, is able to pose as the official exponent of the faith of the Welsh people. Nothing can save a people afflicted by such institutions from the spirit of bondage but an incessant protest against them.

The same observations apply to the question of civil equality. We have not yet attained it in this country—far from it. You will not have established it in this land until the child of the poorest parent shall have the same opportunity for receiving the best education as the child of the richest.

On the other hand, I think there is a danger that Liberals may imagine that their task begins and ends there. If they do so, then they will not accomplish even that task.

The old Liberals in this country used the natural discontent of the people with poverty to win for them a better, more influential and more honourable status in the citizenship of their native land. The new Liberalism, while pursuing this great political ideal with unflinching energy, devotes a part of its endeavour also to the removing of the immediate causes of discontent. It is true that men cannot live by bread alone. It is equally true that a man cannot live without bread. It is a recognition of that elemental fact that has promoted legislation like the Old Age Pensions Act. It is but the beginning of things. Poverty is either the result of a man's own misconduct or misfortune. In so far as he brings it on himself, the State cannot accomplish much. It can do something to protect him. In so far as poverty is due to circumstances over which the man has no control, then the State should step in to the very utmost limit of its resources and save the man from the physical and mental torture involved in extreme penury. The aged we have dealt with during the present Session. We are still confronted with the more gigantic task of dealing with the rest—the sick, the infirm, the unemployed, the widows, and the orphans.

(David Lloyd George in Swansea, 1 October 1908)

[1]
1 When had the *old Liberals* won for the people a *more honourable status in . . . citizenship*? Which (i) adult males, (ii) women were excluded from that *citizenship* in 1908?
2 Gladstone had led the *old Liberals* until 1893. Why did he think that a policy of Free Trade and low taxation would best help the people? Which Radical Liberal wanted the Liberals to do more in 1885?
3 When and how did the Liberals tackle the question of religious equality in Wales? Why did this attempt fail?
4 How and when did the Liberals tackle the question of educational opportunity?

2 Conservative opposition to a welfare system, 1913

It was plain that to take what one man has and to give it to another is unjust, even though the first man may be rich and the second man poor. Do not let us create a privilege for the proletariat, and give a sort of benefit of clergy to trade unions. Could the Conservatives themselves plainly delimit the duty of the State in respect to the relief of suffering?

A more difficult question can scarcely be asked. The poor had no *right* to assistance. The cruel State that leaves a man to starve does not actively injure him. The only question is, does it withhold from him something to which he is entitled? I find it hard to argue that it does. The State helps the poor only for reasons of charity, gratitude for services rendered, or expediency.

And on none of the three grounds has Conservatism any reluctance to support the policy. The only aspect in which these matters can bring Conservatism into conflict with other bodies of opinion is if they are made the occasion of establishing the doctrine that every one has a claim on the State in proportion to the services he has rendered to it. The claim is one of justice, and if admitted as such, a foundation is at once laid on which the fabric of a complete system of State socialism might be erected.

(Robert Cecil, *Conservatism*, 1913)

[2]
1 How had the Liberals given *privileges* and *a sort of benefit* to trade unions in 1906?
2 What were the main differences between Lloyd George and Cecil on *the right* of the poor?
3 How and why would Cecil sometimes provide help for the poor?
4 Why was Cecil opposed to allowing the poor to have *a claim on the State*?

Deprived children

3 Old Age Pensions, 1908

(a) George Cadbury on Old Age Pensions, 1908

We want to see the whole scheme carried out—a shilling a day at sixty for every man and woman in England, from the Duke of Westminster downwards; only with this condition, that if the Duke wants his pension, he must go to the Post Office and get it. If we asked for too much at once, in all human possibility we should have got nothing. Now it is for us to work downwards in the scale of age. There is no work in England so hard as that of the wife of a working man earning 20s. a week. She can never put aside the money for old age pensions and yet she has earned it more than any man living.

(From a speech made in 1908)

(b) Opposition to the Old Age Pensions Act, 1908

The strength of this kingdom, in all its past struggles, has been its great reserve of wealth and the sturdy independent character of its people. The measure which is being pushed through the House of Commons with haste and acclaim will destroy both sources. It will extort the wealth from its possessors by unjust taxation. It will distribute it in small doles, the most wasteful of all forms of expenditure, and will sap the character of the people by teaching them to rely, not on their own exertions, but on the State.

(C. T. Crossthwaite quoted in *The Times*, 3 July 1908)

4 Lloyd George on National Insurance, 1911

What is the explanation that only a portion of the working classes have made provision against sickness and against unemployment? Why? Because very few can afford to pay the premiums, and pay them continuously, which enable a man to provide against those three contingencies. You could not provide against all those three contingencies without paying 1s.6d. or 2s. per week at the very lowest. There are a multitude of the working classes who cannot spare that. Therefore the vast majority choose to insure against death alone. Those who can afford to take up two policies insure against death and sickness, and those who can afford to take up all three insure against death, sickness and unemployment, but only in that order. What are the explanations why they do not insure against all three? Their wages are too low to enable them to insure against all three without some assistance. The second difficulty and it is the greatest of all, is that during a period of sickness or unemployment, when they are earning nothing, they cannot keep up the premiums. They may be able to do it for a fortnight or three weeks, but when times of very bad trade come, arrears run up with the friendly societies. The result is that a very considerable number of workmen find themselves quite unable to keep up the premiums when they have a family to look after. That is the reason why, at the present moment, not one half of the workmen of this country have made any provision for sickness, and not one-tenth for unemployment.

(D. Lloyd George in the House of Commons, 4 May 1911)

[3]
1 How did C. T. Crossthwaite believe that people should provide for their old age? Why did Cadbury argue that this was not possible?
2 When was the first Old Age Pensions Act passed? What were its main terms? How did it differ from the scheme put forward by Cadbury?
3 Why did the first pensioners see their pensions as a *gift*? Why did many of them describe it as 'the Lord George'? Why might they have described it as 'the Lord Asquith'?
4 Why did the pension scheme lead to increases in taxation? Why did it lead to a sharp drop in the level of the Poor Rate?

[4]
1 Which portion of the working classes made some provision against sickness and unemployment? Name two organisations through which they did so.
2 What are *premiums*? Why could the *multitude of the working classes* not afford to provide against *those three contingencies*? Why did some who had begun to pay fail to keep up their payments?
3 Why did the vast majority choose to insure against death? Why did (i) the size of the family, and (ii) the level of the death rate make this more important in 1909 than today?
4 Why did Lloyd George's proposals lead to an increase in taxation?

THE NEW YEAR'S GIFT.

5 Taxation and the welfare state

The Lord Chancellor . . . 'there is ground for thinking that a process of physical deterioration is being threatened among our people. There are things which we have done or which we have promised to do . . . we have made by statute some provision against sweating . . . we have passed an Act for labour exchanges, and we have announced a system of contributory insurance against unemployment, and we hope we may do the same for sickness and disability. We have passed an Act providing for old age pensions. These objects have forced us to ask for the large taxes to which the noble marquis referred. If these taxes are not to be imposed upon income, if death duties are not to be imposed, taxation must fall upon the necessaries of life. That is a policy to which we in this government are wholly opposed. This taxation is not new in the Colonies; it is not new in Germany or in the United States . . .'

(Reported in *The Times*, December 1909)

[5]
1 When and how did the Government become aware that *a process of physical deterioration* threatened the people?
2 What *things* had the Government done about (i) children's health, and (ii) *sweating*?
3 How did reforms associated with (i) Haldane, and (ii) Admiral Fisher also call for *large taxes*?
4 Which taxes did the Government propose to increase? Why was it opposed to *taxation . . . upon the necessaries of life*?

6 Building a new Navy, 1909

In the spring of 1909, the First Lord of the Admiralty, Mr. McKenna, suddenly demanded the construction of no less than six Dreadnought battleships. He based this claim on the rapid growth of the German Fleet. In conjunction with the Chancellor of the Exchequer, I proceeded at once to examine the reasons by which [this scheme] was supported. The conclusions we both reached were that a programme of four ships would sufficiently meet our needs.

The dispute in the Cabinet gave rise to a fierce agitation outside. Genuine alarm was excited throughout the country by what was for the first time widely recognised as a German menace. In the end a curious and characteristic solution was reached. The Admiralty had demanded six ships; the economists had offered four; and we finally compromised on eight.

Whatever differences might be entertained about the exact number of ships required in a particular year, the British Nation in general became conscious of the undoubted fact that Germany proposed to reinforce her unequalled army by a navy which in 1920 would be far stronger than anything up to the present possessed by Great Britain. All sorts of sober-minded people in England began to be profoundly disquieted. What did Germany want this great navy for? There was a growing and deep feeling that the Prussians meant mischief, that they envied the splendour of the British Empire, and if they saw a good chance at our expense, they would take full advantage of it.

(Winston Churchill, *The World Crisis*, 1923)

[6]
1 When and how had Germany started to challenge British naval power before 1909?
2 What type of ships were the *Dreadnought battleships*? Why did they make older battleships obsolete?
3 Who was the *Chancellor of the Exchequer*? Why did he want to build only four ships? What post did Churchill have in the Government in (i) 1909, (ii) 1914?
4 What were the effects of increasing shipbuilding on (i) taxation, and (ii) employment?
5 Why, according to Churchill, did *Germany want this great navy*?

7 The giant-killer

[7]
1 Which tax increase was most opposed by the Irish MPs and brewers?
2 Which tax proposal was most opposed by the owners of land around cities and towns? How did Lloyd George justify this 'incremental tax'? What was the ultimate fate of that proposal?
3 Which tax proposals were most opposed by people earning high incomes? In what ways were Lloyd George's proposals on income tax 'innovative'?
4 When and by whom had death duties been introduced? How did Lloyd George propose to change this form of taxation?
5 Why were Lloyd George's proposals considered (i) too extreme by Gladstonian Liberals, but (ii) too moderate by the Labour Party?

8 The Lords oppose the Budget, 1909

We shall be asked whether we have considered the consequences of rejecting the Budget. What are those consequences? I am told in the first place that there is to be a political deadlock. You will have a Government supported by a huge majority in one House of Parliament, with a minority in the other, and that the Government is deprived for the moment of the control of the purse. Obviously, that would constitute a deadlock. But how long need it last? You hold the key in your own hands. You tell us constantly that you desire to put these issues to the test. Why blame us if we suggest you should do it as soon as possible? Is your Budget so perishable that it will not keep for six weeks?

Then, my Lords, there is a deadlock of another kind. There is a financial deadlock which is described to us in lurid colours. Revenue will cease to come in. There will be no money to pay the troops or to pay old-age pensions, or to pay even the salaries of His Majesty's Ministers. The whole thing is to culminate in a deficit of fifty millions—I think that is the acceptable figure—and in chaos, irreparable chaos. If you don't want to have chaos I am pretty well convinced you need not have it.

There are yet other consequences which we are told to consider. We are told to think well of the consequences to this House. It is in effect intimated to us that as the penalty of rejecting this Bill we are to expect an attempt to deprive this House of its constitutional right of dealing with money Bills. I am not greatly alarmed by these threats. Before the Budget was dreamt of, the same threats were held over our heads. We are therefore justified in assuming that whatever happens, this struggle has got to come. Shall we stand better or shall we stand worse when the struggle comes if we shirk our responsibility now?

(Lord Lansdowne in the House of Lords, 22 November 1909)

9 Lloyd George on the House of Lords

They have slain the Budget. In doing so they have killed the Bill which had in it more promise of better things for the people of this country than most Bills that have been submitted to the House of Commons. It made provision against the inevitable evils which befall such large masses of our poor population—their old age, infirmity, sickness and unemployment. And yet here you have an order of men blessed with every fortune . . . grudging a small pittance out of their super-abundance in order to protect those who have built up their wealth against the haunting terrors of misery and despair.

Well, now, we are on the eve of a General Election, which will decide this great question. Who are the guardians of this mighty people? They are men who have neither the training, the qualifications, nor the experience which would fit them for such a gigantic task . . . they are simply men whose sole qualification is that they are the first-born of persons who had just as little qualifications as themselves.

(D. Lloyd George, speech, December 1909)

[8, 9]

1 Which parts of the 1909 Budget were particularly offensive to the Lords?

2 What *test* did Lansdowne have in mind? When did this take place? What was the result? What happened to this Budget after that *test*?

3 What were the effects of depriving the Government of the control of the purse? Why did Lloyd George consider this to be unjust?

4 Why did Lansdowne earn the nickname of 'Hedger' in 1911?

Topic 14 Parliamentary Reform, 1865–1912

1 John Bright on Reform, 1865

The Tories, and those Whigs who are like Tories, have an uncomfortable feeling. They are afraid of the five or six million grown-up men who are allowed to marry, to earn their living, who pay taxes—they are afraid of the five or six million who by the present system of representation are shut out from the commonest rights of citizenship. An Englishman, if he goes to the Cape, to Australia or to the Canadian Federation, can vote. It is only in his own country that he is denied this right which in every other community of Englishmen in the world would be freely accorded to him.

This state of things I hold to be dangerous. It was so in the years 1831–32. There are men in this room who felt then, and know now, that it required but an accident—and this country would have been in the throes of revolution.

It was not democracy in 1832 that was the peril. It was the desperate antagonism of the class that then had power to the just claims and rights of the people. And at this moment, that Conservatism, be it Tory or Whig, is the true national peril which we have to face. They may dam the stream, they may keep back the waters, but the volume is ever increasing, and it descends with accelerated force, and the time will come when, if wisdom does not take the place of folly, the waters will burst their banks and these men, who fancy they are stemming this imaginary apparition of democracy, will be swept away by the resolute will of a united and determined people.

(John Bright speaking in Birmingham Town Hall, 18 January 1865)

[1]
1 Which Whig was Prime Minister when Bright made his speech? What did Bright mean by describing him and other Whigs as being *like Tories*? Why was this unfair to the then leaders of the Tory Party?
2 Which class dominated the electorate in 1865? Which class might have led a revolution in 1831–2? Which class had dominated the electorate in 1831–2?
3 How did the majority of MPs show their attitude towards proposals such as Bright's in (i) 1859, (ii) 1866?

2 Gladstone proposes Reform, 1866

Since 1832 every kind of beneficial change has been in operation in favour of the working classes. It is hardly an exaggeration to say that within that time the civilising powers of education have . . . been . . . brought into existence as far as the mass of the people is concerned. I will not believe that the mass of Gentlemen opposite are really insensible to the enormous benefit that has been effected by that emancipation of the press, when for the humble sum of a penny, or even less, newspapers are circulated from day to day by the million rather than by the thousand, carrying home to all classes of our fellow-countrymen accounts of public affairs. And there is not a call which has been made

[2]
1 How had the working class proved to Gladstone that they were fit to vote? Was Gladstone asking for universal suffrage? Explain your answer.
2 What evidence is there here that the standards of living of the working class were rising in the 1860s? How do you account for that rise?

upon the self-improving powers of the working community, which has not been fully answered. Take, for instance, the Working Men's Free Libraries and Institutes throughout the country . . . take, as an example of the class, Liverpool; who are the frequenters of that institution? I believe that the majority of the careful students who crowd that library are men belonging to the working classes. Then again, sir, we instituted for them Post Office Savings Banks, which may now be said to have been in full operation for four years; and what has been the result? There are now 650,000 depositors in those savings banks.

But what is the meaning of all this? Parliament has been striving to make the working classes progressively fitter and fitter for the franchise; and can anything be more unwise, not to say more senseless, than to persevere from year to year in this plan, and then blindly to refuse to recognise its legitimate upshot—namely, the increased fitness of the working classes for the exercise of political power?

(Speech in the House of Commons, 12 April 1866)

3 What part had Gladstone played in (i) the *emancipation of the press*, (ii) the establishment of the Post Office Savings Bank? Why were these reforms beneficial to only a minority of the working class?
4 How did the existence of the trade union movement reflect the *self-improving powers of the working community*?

3 Robert Lowe opposes his party's Reform Bill, 1866

If the Bill is passed it is certain that sooner or later we shall see the working classes in majority in the constituencies. Look what that implies. I shall speak very frankly on this subject.

Let any Gentleman consider the constituencies he has had the honour to be concerned with. If you want venality, if you want ignorance, if you want drunkenness, and facility for being intimidated; or if, on the other hand, you want impulsive, unreflecting, and violent people, where do you look for them in the constituencies? Do you go to the top or to the bottom?

I ask the House to consider what good we are to get for the country at large by this reduction of the franchise? The working men of England, finding themselves in a full majority of the whole constituency will awake to a full sense of their power. They will say 'We can do better for ourselves. Don't let us any longer be cajoled at elections. Let us set up shop for ourselves. We have objects to serve as well as our neighbours, and let us unite to carry out those objects. We have machinery; we have our trade unions; we have our leaders all ready . . . ' Well, when that is the case—when you have a Parliament appointed, as it will be, by such constituencies so deteriorated—with a pressure of that kind brought to bear, what is it you expect Parliament to stop at? Where is the line to be drawn?

(Speech in House of Commons, 13 March 1866)

[3]
1 What did Lowe believe would happen in the constituencies if working men were given the vote? Have you any evidence that *venality . . . drunkenness . . . intimidation* existed before this? To what extent did Acts passed in (i) 1872, and (ii) 1883 help to change the pattern of elections?
2 Which party was founded when working men first decided to *set up shop* for themselves? When did they first do so? Who was their first leader?
3 How had the behaviour of (i) the aristocracy before 1820, and (ii) the middle classes in the 1840s indicated that those who had power had *objects to serve*?
4 Why did attempts to find the answer to Lowe's final question (i) divide the Liberals in 1885, (ii) lead to the development of New Liberalism after 1906?
5 Why was Lowe able to play a part in the defeat of Gladstone's Bill in 1866 but unable to prevent the passage of Disraeli's Bill in 1867?

4 The Ballot Act, 1872

Sir,

We are to have a ballot at last, after forty years' struggle for it. The power of the Lords and of like scamps in the Commons has been hitherto so great against the people, that the latter have all these years been asking in vain that their property over their opinions may remain their own. With the ballot, farmers will be better able to return a different sort of men to the House of Commons.

But we must go on and get more. We must have a redistribution of seats. It will never do to let a little town like Tamworth, with 10,000 inhabitants including its hamlets, return two members, while Birmingham, with 350,000 people returns only three.

We shall not have honest laws until many landowners are replaced by working men; be they mechanics, traders, farmers or labourers, I don't mind who, so that they will make honest laws.

(*Reynolds' News*, 21 July 1872)

A Jew voting by ballot

[4]

1 Why did the system of voting before 1872 allow the *Lords and like scamps* to influence the voting behaviour of many workers?

2 Why was a ballot an essential part of the development of the democratic process?

3 Why did the ballot lead to the election of more nationalistic minded MPs in Ireland? Which Irish political leader took advantage of this change in Irish politics?

4 Why was the question of a ballot more important in 1872 than it had been forty years earlier?

5 How was the *power of the Lords* to control elections further diminished by an Act passed in 1883?

6 When was the next *redistribution of seats* after 1872? Who insisted on this redistribution? Why?

5 The demands of labour, 1892

(John Burns, writing in the year in which Keir Hardie was elected to Parliament, put forward the demands of the working-class voters.)

The world moves on its belly; and politicians will find that the people have longer memories than formerly, especially when the possessors of the empty bellies have votes. We are passing through a transition period. Laissez-faire has been abandoned, and for the first time in the history of the human race the working people possess universally the power through elective institutions to embody in law their economic and material desires. Concurrently with the growth of personal independence is the desire for State and municipal effort when individual action is futile. It is the protest of labour against charitable palliation of a social system that in all countries is breaking up and must either by force or steady change . . . give place to the organised and collective domination by the people of their social life through municipal administration and political change.

[5]

1 Which sections of the people did not have votes in 1892?

2 Which MP claimed to speak for *labour* in 1892? Which MPs challenged his right to do so?

3 Why was there an increase in the number of *empty bellies* in the 1890s? How did (i) Salisbury, and (ii) Gladstone propose to help *possessors* of those bellies?

4 How did the workers try to use their industrial power to satisfy their *economic and material desires*?

6 Labour and Elections

In October my wife and I went to America to give a short series of lectures. We were in Pittsburg when the news came of the breakdown of the Conference and the government's decision to dissolve Parliament. The American newspapers gave alarmist reports of the political crisis in England, and one evening newspaper in Pittsburg came out with a front-page scarehead in letters an inch deep: 'Revolution in England! King George in flight?' The only foundation for the startling news that the King was in flight was that he was on his way from Balmoral to London to be in close touch with his Ministers. I had to make arrangements to return to England at once.

When I emerged from the station [at Blackburn] to my amazement the great square outside was packed by a dense crowd. The route through the principal streets to the market-place was marked by scenes of unprecedented enthusiasm. It was a great start for our Election campaign, which a week later ended in a triumphant victory. This contest was fought exclusively on the House of Lords issue.

For the second time within twelve months the country had decided the issue of The Peers versus The People. The Government had received a very definite mandate from the country to place the Parliament Bill upon the Statute Book with the least possible delay. The Liberals and Labour and the Nationalists combined had a majority of 126 over the Unionists. Owing to unpreparedness, the Labour Party put forward only 56 candidates at this General Election [December 1910], and 42 were returned. It had been very greatly hampered by a recent decision of the House of Lords which had declared it to be illegal for trade unionists to spend the funds of their organisations on political work.

(Philip Viscount Snowden, *An Autobiography*, vol. 1, 1934)

[6]

1 Of which year was Snowden writing?

2 Where had *the Conference* been held? Why did it suffer a breakdown?

3 How far was the report of *Revolution in England* supported by reports of the behaviour of (i) women, (ii) trade unionists, (iii) Ulster Protestants?

4 In which month did *the Election* take place? Why did it resemble a referendum? What was the Liberal slogan during the election campaign?

5 Why was the support of the *Nationalists* (i) essential to the *Liberals*, (ii) more important than that of *Labour*?

6 Which *decision of the House of Lords* affected the Labour Party during this election?

7 How did the Liberals reward their allies by Acts passed in (i) 1911, (ii) 1912, (iii) 1913?

7 The Parliament Bill, 1911

Whereas it is expedient that provision should be made for regulating the relations between the two Houses of Parliament.

And whereas it is intended to substitute for the House of Lords as it at present exists, a Second Chamber constituted on a popular instead of hereditary basis, but such substitution cannot be immediately brought into operation:

Be it therefore enacted by the King's most excellent Majesty, etc.

I(i) If a Money Bill having been passed by the House of Commons, and sent up to the House of Lords at least one month before the end of the session, is not passed by the House of Lords without amendment within one month after it is so sent up to the House, the Bill shall . . . be presented to His Majesty and become an Act of Parliament on the Royal Assent being signified.

II(i) If any Public Bill (other than a Money Bill or a Bill containing any provision to extend the maximum duration of Parliament beyond five years) is passed by the House of Commons in three successive sessions . . . and having been sent up to the House of Lords at least one month before the end of the Session, is rejected by the House of Lords . . . that Bill shall on its rejection for the third time by the House of Lords . . . be presented to His Majesty and become an Act of Parliament.

8 Who's afraid?

[7, 8]

1 Which of the powers of the Lords were (i) lessened, (ii) taken away completely? Why was their power after 1911 described as that of a 'suspensive veto'?

2 Which portion of this Act has never been acted on? Why has the Commons been reluctant to act on it?

3 When was the Home Rule Bill introduced by the Asquith Government? Why was it guaranteed approval by the Commons?

4 How was the Bill treated when it went to the Lords? Why is it shown as sheltering behind the Parliament Act?

5 In which year was the Home Rule Bill *presented to His Majesty*? Why? Why did all parties agree not to put the Act into operation immediately?

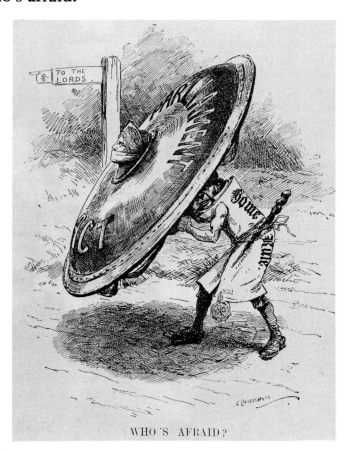

WHO'S AFRAID?

Topic 15 Steps Towards War, 1890–1914

1 The position in 1892

The situation for some years had been this: that the two restless Powers in Europe were France and Russia; that is, they were the two Powers from whom trouble to the peace of Europe was expected, if at all. The solid quiet group in Europe at that time was the Triple Alliance. It had been the policy of Lord Salisbury before 1892, and it was the policy of Mr. Gladstone's Government of 1892, not to join the Triple Alliance or come under definite commitment to it, but generally in diplomacy to side with the Triple Alliance as being the stable Power in Europe, and the one which was securing the peace. It was not very comfortable, even so far as Germany was concerned; but as regards Russia and France, the situation was very much worse.

(Extract from the minutes of the Committee of Imperial Defence at a meeting of 26 May 1911)

2 Chamberlain on an alliance with the USA, 1898

I desire, most earnestly desire, a close, a cordial and intimate connection with the United States of America. Will anyone say that the occasion may not arise . . . that Anglo-Saxon liberty and Anglo-Saxon interests may hereafter be menaced by a greater combination of other Powers? I think that such a thing is possible, and in that case . . . I hope that blood will be thicker than water.

They are our kinsfolk. Our imagination must be fired when we contemplate the possibility of cordial understanding between the seventy millions who inhabit the United States of America and the fifty millions of Britons which inhabit the United Kingdom and the Colonies of the Queen. A combination of that kind would be a guarantee for the peace and civilisation of the world.

(Quoted in J. L. Garvin and J. Amery, *The Life of Joseph Chamberlain*, 1932)

3 Chamberlain on an alliance with Germany, 1898

The natural alliance is between ourselves and the great German Empire. We have had our differences with Germany. I cannot conceive any point which can arise in the immediate future which would bring ourselves and the Germans into antagonism of interests. If the union between England and America is a powerful factor in the cause of peace, a new Triple Alliance between the Teutonic race and the two great branches of the Anglo-Saxon race, will be a still more potent influence in the future of the world.

(Garvin and Amery, *The Life of Joseph Chamberlain*)

[1]
1 Why was France *restless* after 1871? Where and why did British interests in Africa clash with those of France in (i) 1881–2, (ii) 1898?
2 Why was Russia a source of trouble to Britain in (i) Central Asia, and (ii) the Far East between 1880 and 1900?
3 Which countries formed the Triple Alliance? Explain which was the most likely to become involved in a clash with (i) Russia, (ii) France in Europe, (iii) France in Africa.
4 When did France and Russia form a Dual Alliance? What was surprising about this development?

[2, 3]
1 What position did Chamberlain have in the Government in 1898? Who was Foreign Secretary in that government?
2 In which war was the United States involved in 1898? Why did this involvement please British imperialists?
3 Why was it both incorrect and insulting to many Americans to refer continually to the *Anglo-Saxon interests* of the United States?
4 What was 'natural' about an alliance with Germany? Who had proposed and who had rejected such an alliance earlier in the 1890s?
5 Which laws passed in Germany in 1898 and 1900 led to increased tension between Germany and Great Britain? What response did Britain make to those laws in 1909?

4 Chamberlain and the lessons of the Boer War, 1900

The war has brought the Empire closer together. During that great struggle, Great Britain stood alone, isolated among the greater nations of the world. The lesson to all is our strength in unity. It has taught us that we no longer stand alone, it has laid upon us the duty of maintaining and strengthening the friendships which we have learnt to value. The splendid, and above all, the spontaneous rally of the Colonies to the Mother Country affords no slight compensation even for the sufferings of war. What has brought them to your side even before you called upon them? It is that ... these peoples for the first time claim their share in the duties and responsibilities as well as in the privileges of Empire. We are advancing steadily, if slowly, to the realisation of that great federation of our race which will inevitably make for peace and liberty and justice.

(Garvin and Amery, *The Life of Joseph Chamberlain*)

[4]
1 Which countries in the Empire had sent troops to help Britain? From which country had Britain ordered troops to be sent?
2 Why was Chamberlain justified in describing the Boer War as a *great struggle*? Why had it lasted so long?
3 How had the German Kaiser encouraged the Boers in 1895? Why did Britain bear this in mind when Germany began to build a large navy?
4 What *lesson* had Britain learned about her ability to *stand alone*?

5 The Entente, 1904

The Anglo-French Agreement of 1904 ... at once removed all risk of a quarrel between the United Kingdom and France, and brought the two nations to realise that there was no reason why they should not be the best of friends.

Then, after the bitterness of the Russo-Japanese war had disappeared, the same policy was pursued with Russia.

Now, that is the situation. We do not need to pursue any policy of ambition in Europe. The cause of anxiety now as regards Germany arises entirely from the question of the German naval expenditure, which is very considerable, and which, if it is increased, will produce an impression on the world at large that the object of Germany is to build a fleet which shall be bigger than the British fleet. If she had a fleet bigger than the British fleet, obviously she could be in London in a very short time with her army. But however much our fleet is superior to the German fleet, with the army we have we could never commit a serious agression by ourselves upon German territory.

(Committee of Imperial Defence, 26 May 1911)

[5]
1 Why did France think that the Dual Alliance was weaker in 1904 than it had seemed to be in 1900? How did this influence French opinion about an understanding with England?
2 What issues were settled in the Agreement concerning (i) Egypt, and (ii) Morocco?
3 How had the Russo-Japanese war (i) shown Russia that France was not a reliable ally, (ii) shown Britain that Russia was not to be feared?
4 Why did the building of a large German navy give Germany a preponderance of power in Europe?

6 The Landing of William II in Tangier, 31 March 1905

There was a very fitting reception on the dock by officials and the German colony. Then a ride through the gaily decorated streets amid the indescribable joy of the natives and the European population. In the Embassy there was a reception of Germans, the diplomatic corps, and the Sultan's envoy, who had not been able to come aboard ship.

In conversing with the French agent, when the latter conveyed his respects and greetings from Delcassé, the Kaiser replied that his visit meant that His Majesty wanted free trade for Germany and complete equality of rights with other countries. When Count Cherisey was about to acknowledge these remarks courteously, His Majesty said that

[6]
1 In which country was Tangier? Who was the Sultan?
2 Who was Delcassé? Why was he forced to resign in 1905?
3 Why did the French agent, Count Cherisey, think that he had the right to *acknowledge these remarks*? What was the significance of His Majesty's determination to negotiate directly with the Sultan?

he would like to treat directly with the Sultan, the free ruler of an independent country, as an equal; that he himself would be able to make his just claims valid, and that he expected that these claims would also be recognised by France. Count Cherisey became pale. He was about to respond, but was curtly dismissed.

Reception of the honourable great uncle of the Sultan was very formal. His Majesty remarked that he looked upon the Sultan as the ruler of a free and independent empire subject to no foreign control; that he expected Germany to have advantages equal to those of other countries in trade and commerce; and that he himself would always negotiate directly with the Sultan.

(Report of Councillor von Schoen to the German Foreign Office)

4 Why did the Sultan call for a conference following this visit? Why did France want to refuse such a request? Where and when did the conference take place?
5 What was the outcome of the conference with regard to (i) French power over the Sultan, and (ii) the continuity of British policy under opposing political parties?

7 The 1911 crisis

Suddenly, on the morning of July 1st, it was announced that His Imperial Majesty had sent his gunboat, the Panther, to Agadir. France found herself in the presence of an act which could not be explained . . . Great Britain began to wonder what bearing a naval base on the Atlantic Coast of Africa would have upon her maritime security. The Ministers conducting the foreign policy of Britain, were drawn entirely from the Liberal Imperialist section of the Government. They were narrowly watched and kept in equipoise by the Radical element. In these circumstances the attitude of the Chancellor of the Exchequer became of peculiar importance.

That night [21st July] [he] used the following words: 'If a situation were to be forced upon us in which peace could only be preserved by the surrender of the great position Britain has won by centuries of heroism and achievement, by allowing Britain to be treated as if she were of no account in the Cabinet of nations, then I say emphatically that peace at that price would be a humiliation intolerable for a great country like ours to endure.'

Four days later, at about 5.30 in the afternoon, the Chancellor of the Exchequer and I were walking by the fountains of Buckingham Palace. Hot foot on our track came a messenger. Will the Chancellor of the Exchequer go at once to Sir Edward Grey? We found Sir Edward Grey in his rooms at the House of Commons. His first words were 'I have just received a communication from the German Ambassador so stiff that the Fleet might be attacked at any moment. I have sent for McKenna to warn him!'

He then told us of [his] conversation with Count Metternich. The Ambassador read a long complaint about Mr. Lloyd George's speech which had been interpreted by the presses of Great Britain and France as a warning 'bordering on menace'. Sir Edward Grey had thought it right to reply that the tone of the communication rendered it inconsistent with the dignity of His Majesty's Government to give explanations. The First Lord arrived while we were talking, and a few minutes later hurried off to send the warning orders.

(Winston Churchill, *The World Crisis*, 1923)

[7]
1 Where is Agadir? In which year was it a centre of an international crisis?
2 Why was *France* more involved in Moroccan affairs than had been agreed at Algeciras?
3 Why did the German seizure of Agadir break the terms of the Algeciras agreement? Why did this offend *Sir Edward Grey*?
4 Why did Germany interpret the Chancellor's speech as '*bordering on menace*'? Why did it please (i) *Grey*, and (ii) *France*?
5 Why was this crisis more serious than that of 1905?

8 Malgré elle

THE MATCH-MAKER MALGRÉ ELLE.

Mlle. La France (*aside*). "IF SHE'S GOING TO GLARE AT US LIKE THAT, IT ALMOST LOOKS
AS IF WE MIGHT HAVE TO BE REGULARLY ENGAGED."

9 Britain and France draw closer together

My dear Ambassador,

From time to time in recent years the French and British naval and military experts have consulted together. It has always been understood that such consultation does not restrict the freedom of either Government to decide at any future time whether or not to assist the other by armed force. We have agreed that consultation between experts is not, and ought not to be regarded as an engagement that commits either Government to action in a contingency that has not arisen and may never arise. The disposition, for instance, of the French and British fleets respectively at the present moment is not based upon an engagement to co-operate in war.

You have, however, pointed out that, if either Government had grave reason to expect an unprovoked attack by a third Power, it might become essential to know whether it could in that event depend upon the armed assistance of the other.

I agree that, if either Government had grave reason to expect an unprovoked attack by a third Power, or something that threatened the general peace, it should immediately discuss with the other whether both Governments should act together to prevent aggression and to preserve peace, and, if so, what measures they would be prepared to take in common. If these measures involved action, the plans of the General Staffs would at once be taken into consideration and the Governments would then decide what effect should be given to them.

Yours, etc.,

22 November 1912   E. Grey

[8, 9]

1 When had *the French and British military experts* first begun to hold meetings? What was the purpose of such meetings? Why did they lead to the formation of a British Expeditionary Force?

2 When had *French and British naval experts* first begun to have meetings? What arrangements did they make for the disposition of the fleets of both countries?

3 How did these discussions and arrangements tend to change the nature of the *Entente Cordiale*? Which party in the *Entente* did the cartoonist think was most anxious for the *Entente* to become a formal alliance?

4 How did France show herself to be an unreliable ally to Russia in (i) 1904, (ii) 1908?

5 How far do you think Germany was to blame for the increased tension with Britain after 1900? What answer might be given to the German complaint that in 1914 'we were encircled'?

10 War or peace? July–August 1914

The Cabinet was overwhelmingly pacific. At least three-quarters of its members were determined not to be drawn into a European quarrel, unless Great Britain herself were attacked, and were inclined to believe first that Austria and Serbia would not come to blows; secondly, that if they did Russia would not intervene; thirdly, if Russia intervened that Germany would not strike; fourthly they hoped France and Germany [would] neutralise each other without fighting. They did not believe that if Germany attacked France, she would attack her through Belgium. It was not until August 3rd that the appeal from the King of the Belgians for French and British aid raised an issue which united the Ministers and enabled Sir Edward Grey to make his speech to the House of Commons.

(Winston Churchill, *The World Crisis*, 1923)

11 Grey in the Commons, 3 August 1914

The present crisis has originated in a dispute between Austria and Serbia. No Government has less desire to be involved in war over a dispute with Austria and Serbia than the Government and the country of France. They are involved in it because of their alliance with Russia. That obligation cannot apply to us. We are not parties to the Franco-Russian Alliance. I now come to what we think the situation requires of us. For many years we have had a long-standing friendship with France. But how far that friendship entails obligation . . . let every man look into his own heart. The French fleet is now in the Mediterranean, and the Northern and Western coasts of France are absolutely undefended. My own feeling is that if a foreign fleet engaged in a war which France had not sought . . . came down the English Channel and bombarded the undefended coasts of France, we could not stand aside.

Yesterday afternoon I gave to the French Ambassador the following statement:

'I am authorised to give an assurance that if the German Fleet comes into the Channel or through the North Sea to undertake hostile operations against the French coasts or shipping the British Fleet will give all the protection in its power.'

And, Sir, there is the more serious consideration . . . the neutrality of Belgium. When mobilisation was beginning I telegraphed to both Paris and Berlin to say that it was essential for us to know whether the French and German Governments were prepared to respect the neutrality of Belgium. I got from the French Government this reply:

'The French Government are resolved to respect the neutrality of Belgium.'

From the German Government the reply was that:

The German Minister for Foreign Affairs . . . rather doubted whether they could give an answer at all, as any reply they might give could not fail, in the event of war, to have the undesirable effect of disclosing, to a certain extent, part of their plan of campaign.

[10]

1 What office did Churchill hold in the Cabinet in August 1914? Which members of the *pacific* Cabinet resigned on the outbreak of war?
2 Why did the memory of the events of 1908 lead some of the Cabinet to hope that *Russia would not intervene*? Why was Russia stronger in 1914 than she had been in 1908?
3 What names do we give to the relationships between (i) Austria and Germany, and (ii) Russia and France? How did these relationships differ from Britain's relationship with European Powers in July 1914?
4 Why did this encourage three-quarters of the Cabinet to hope that Britain would *not . . . be drawn into a European quarrel*?
5 Which German 'Plan' led to the invasion of Belgium? Why did Germany concentrate her initial effort against France and not Russia?

12 A scrap of paper

The German Chancellor to the British Ambassador to Germany, 4 August 1914:

The step taken by Britain because of our infringement of the neutrality of Belgium was terrible to a degree. Just for a word, neutrality; just for a scrap of paper, Great Britain is going to make war on a kindred nation which desired nothing better than to be friends with her. It is unthinkable. It was like striking a man from behind while he is fighting for his life against two assailants.

13 Germany and Belgium

The German Chancellor to the Reichstag, 4 August 1914:

It would have been disastrous to have waited for the French attack. So we invaded Belgium. Gentlemen, we are now in a state of necessity, and necessity knows no law. The invasion is a violation of international law. But this wrong will be remedied when our military aims have been attained. Anyone who is menaced as we are can consider only how he is to hack his way through.

(Items 12 and 13 adapted from Nicholas Mansergh, *The Coming of the First World War*, 1949)

14 King George V to the American Ambassador in London, 4 August 1914

My God, Mr. Page, what else could we do?

15 Sir Edward Grey on the evening of 4 August 1914

The lamps are going out all over Europe: we shall not see them lit again in our lifetime.

[11, 12, 13, 14, 15]

1 When and why did *the present crisis* begin? How had it been worsened by Austrian demands on Serbia?

2 Why did Russia become involved in the crisis? How did Germany react to Russian behaviour in July 1914? Why? Why did France become involved in *the crisis*?

3 Whose interests would be safeguarded by the concentration of the *French fleet* in the Mediterranean? Why did Britain prefer to concentrate her fleet in the Atlantic?

4 How might the German navy have taken advantage of the absence of a *French fleet* from *the Northern and Western coasts of France*? Why did this impose an *obligation* of honour on Britain in 1914?

5 Why did the announcement of these arrangements come as a complete surprise to most of the Cabinet and to nearly all MPs?

6 When did the European powers guarantee the *neutrality* of Belgium? How had Germany treated that guarantee in the war of 1870–1? What did Germany demand from Belgium on 3 August 1914? How did the German Chancellor justify the invasion of Belgium?

7 Who were the *two assailants*? How far was this a correct description?